# A Dancer's Final Bow

## Louise Salisbury

LitPrime Solutions
485c US Highway 1 South
Suite 100
Iselin, NJ 08830
www.litprime.com
Phone: 1-800-981-9893

Published by LitPrime Solutions: 08/15/2024

ISBN: 979-8-88703-396-9(sc)
ISBN: 979-8-88703-397-6(e)

Library of Congress Control Number: 2024916433

Any people depicted in stock imagery provided by iStock are models, and such images are being used for illustrative purposes only.

Certain stock imagery © iStock.

Because of the dynamic nature of the Internet, any web addresses or links contained in this book may have changed since publication and may no longer be valid. The views expressed in this work are solely those of the author and do not necessarily reflect the views of the publisher, and the publisher hereby disclaims any responsibility for them.

For Jason and Elektra

My True Loves

## Yesterday

Chokecherries

The Blue Dress

Grace Hill

Manners

The Christmas Present

The Map

The Cherry Coke

Ten

Daddy

Playground

Green

High School

Maternity

Shaft

The Boarders

The Body

# Chokecherries

If I went back it wouldn't be for another glimpse of familiar faces, kind, well-meaning, unrecognizing, oblivious. It would be to ferret out the chokecherry, bitter, black, insistent, suspended in clusters but in no other way resembling the sweet, juicy, practical grape. I would have to hunt through Cheyenne Canyon, avoiding (yet tempted to plunge into the middle of) the wayward beds of poison ivy, to find the curving green leaves receding from civilization, headed the way of the buffalo, the nomad, the moccasined. I would have to strip a handful of the stone-centered berries, to eat them in remembrance, leaving a tattooed hand and lips. I would stand alum-mouthed in disbelief at the impact.

To my mother I am indebted. She had the patience, the stamina, to turn the ink-like juice into jelly. Buckets of the frugal fruit were required for a pint or two of jelly. No pectin but cups of sugar were necessary to mediate the bitter.

We children, with Daddy along to tell us what was or wasn't poison ivy, foraged through the brush following the stream upwards, picking pailsful of Rocky Mountain cherries. I had moccasins and pemmican on my mind and tried not to rustle a leaf or snap a twig. I was certain deer lived here, was certain at another time I did. I did not want to disturb the holy woods, but, nonetheless, we took the harvest like sorry thieves, silently, without blandishment.

At home my mother ripped a sheet, the sound tearing the air worse than the fabric. The washed, boiled berries were put into it like fresh meat and squeezed, but the rock hard pits didn't yield much. Mother left the bag hanging in the middle of the kitchen, suspended from a wooden clothes rack, as if to eke a confession out of it drip by drip. We walked around it. The white sheet turned a vivid war-paint red, drying to purple later.

The ultimate jelly was savory, rare, speaking chokecherry like a native, telling the moccasined to get ready for what was to come. Telling them not to give up. Telling them to remember what chokecherry meant. That is why I would have to go back, to see if the canyon is still talking like that, or if it was just my imagination.

# The Blue Dress

The dress was cerulean that favored blue, deep-set and solemn. It had been turned into a little girl's dress by a babysitter's fondness. An old German given to baby talk. "Her's sure going to look pretty in her new blue dress, her is."

The dress lay in state on the walnut table. The tissue paper pattern was pinned on top like a mysterious map to the seamstress' destination. The scalloped edge made it slow going for Mrs. Hill and her straight pins. Careful. Careful in the cutting. The elegant velvet wanted to wander from the scissors' sharp edge. Pinking shears were no help at all when it came to velvet, Mrs. Hill said.

The blue dress was made of remnants from her daughter's trio dresses. The trio sang for the boys at Fort Carson wearing bright red lipstick, big smiles, and high heels. Close harmonies like the McGuire sisters kept the trio practicing and sets of three matching dresses kept Mrs. Hill sewing. But this dress was different, not an obligation but a thrifty whim. Something for the youngest, her little Loweezy, a Sunday best.

There wasn't enough blue velvet so the bodice had to wait. Crab apple butter was put up. Vegetables from the garden progressed from weeded rows, to bushel baskets, to the back porch, to a boiling water bath, only to end up in rows again, this time on shelves in the cellar. Lodged in sparkling jars with screw top lids were red tomatoes and green tomato preserves, yellow corn and summer squash, Royal Anne cherries and dark purple plums. The purple having been coaxed back towards blue. The blue of the waiting bodice, the idle velvet afterthought.

Then a troop of soldiers was about to be shipped overseas and some new scraps of taffeta showed up. A silvery sheen nestled among cobalt prisms. A match was made. The project Mrs. Hill feared had been scrapped was resumed.

Puffed sleeves appeared, and a gathered skirt with a sash. Mrs. Hill stood little Loweezy on a chair and pinned up the hem.

Then it was ready for buttons. An event in itself, requiring money to be spent. They took a trip to Penney's after a penny went into the parking meter. They walked past the voluminous half-slips like an explosion of carnations, then (watch your step) up the escalator craning your neck for a final glimpse of the half-slips, then (watch your step again) and they were in Fabrics.

Bolts and bolts of color and pastels. Aisles of prints, chintz, corduroy, cotton, linen, twill, paisley, muslin, wool, soft flannel, bold plaid, crinkly seersucker, and scratchy but ethereal organdy. They walked past all that and on to Notions with the rickety swiveling button rack. Buttons made of gold, silver, wood, bone. Buttons in the shape of ducks, bows, anchors, medallions. But for the blue dress a tiny ebony button with a silver rim was chosen. "Perfect," they said. These were made for the dress. It was unanimous. Mrs. Hill opened her pocketbook.

The blue dress was christened on Easter by a Kodak camera. A smile of equanimity donned the velvet. Honored, little Loweezy felt like a movie star.

# Grace Hill

Grace Hill had African violets that bloomed covered with dust. She had very little hair, and my mother used to put it up in pin curls that looked like little black snails on a white scalp with precision X's where the bobby pins went.

On the mantle sat a pink marble lighthouse. I climbed the steps with my fingers one by one and sang "Jesus Loves the Little Children." The lighthouse was fleshy pink like her corset that laced cat's cradle from beneath her hips to her armpits.

Mrs. Hill made soap, and I was told frightening things about the effects of lye which intrigued me. She had a vegetable garden and troweled the huge, one-eyed, green-bleeding tomato worms in half without losing speed. Buttercups grew down by the creek. I pressed against the fence but couldn't get to them.

Mr. Hill grunted and limped. I slammed my finger in the door and looked down to see my nail float off in a pool of blood. Daddy saidpoor girl and took me home.

Grace made me a blue velvet dress for Christmas. When Daddy took my picture in it, I looked like Barbara Stanwyck.

Lois was Grace Hill's daughter. I adored her. She could stand on her head and had a picture of Wally on the dresser. She plucked her eyebrows and insisted it didn't hurt. I didn't believe her. She had lots of full skirts in her closet and rows of high heels perched on a rack. My sister and I scratched her back with brushes. She moaned lowly.

Lois washed her feet in the sink which I thought was sexy. Ten years later, when I was tall enough to stick my foot in the sink, I tried it. My father caught me and screamed furiously, "I knew it was coming to this!"

# Manners

You must forgive me. Perhaps I was too young to remember accurately. It was the macaroni and cheese that reminded me of it, particularly when I was scrubbing the baked-on crust off the dish. I remembered her wrists half submerged in grey dishwater, all the way up to the bandages that circled them, although I was too young to know anything about it. I didn't even have a word to call the ominous feeling that surrounded that evening.

I had been invited to dinner at a neighbor girl's house, my first dinner away from home. It felt strange sitting down in someone else's kitchen. So much was the same, yet so different, a mother and father, not mine, a brother and sister, also strangers. I didn't even know their names.

The light bulb over the kitchen table seemed blinding and made the night outside the windows even blacker. I wondered how I would ever find my way home in the dark. I was terrified. Maybe I should make a dash for it right that minute, just get up and run, but I knew I could never do that. It wouldn't be good manners. Besides, everyone was already seated around the table. I had no idea what I was doing there, except that in my family it was some sort of honor to receive an invitation anywhere for any reason. It meant something very important. It meant you weren't all bad. An invitation had to be accepted, like a dare, or you were chicken. So there I sat, waiting for dinner, the quiet-as-a-mouse girl from five houses down.

Then something comforting happened. Two hands behind potholders reached forward to place a hot dish on the table. It was macaroni and cheese, an old favorite, with something I didn't recognize sprinkled on top. I asked what it was and was told, breadcrumbs. I felt encouraged. At least I would be able to eat what was served.

As the mother's arms were extended towards the center of the table, all eyes were on her hands in the act of setting the dish down. The girl and her brother started to giggle and pointed to her wrists, all taped up on the insides with white gauze, as if something really bad had happened there. I remember thinking whatever it was, it must have hurt. I couldn't see what there was to laugh about.

I watched the mother whose expression never changed, a woman so quiet I wondered if she even knew how to talk. It was uncomfortable sitting next to the giggling, pointing girl and her go-along-with-it brother. They were trying to tell me what had happened to the wrists, something about making X's on them. She had done it herself, they pursued, enjoying my density, asking if I understood what they were talking about. I said I did to make them stop it and eat their macaroni. Whatever they were getting at, I didn't want to know. I just wanted to go back home where I knew what to expect. I thought my mother might like to know about the breadcrumbs on top, but then I figured she'd say it was just a garnish.

I wanted to stick up for the mother who didn't scold her rude children, but she was so quiet it made me sad. So sad I asked to be excused right after dinner and ran all the way home, pounding my heels into the cement with each step, forgetting to be afraid of the dark, feeling more and more alive the further away I got from the silent serving woman and the cruel, joking children. Before I left I remembered my manners, so I said, "Thanks for the dinner." She smiled and said, "Come again." We understood each other.

# The Christmas Present

It was below freezing on a Christmas Eve, the wind whipped around her bare knees. The wool coat buttoned to her chin was in no way adequate to the wind. The traffic lights swung alarmingly like charms on a bracelet. The tinsel garlands dangled in strips where once they had stretched like a canopy across the street.

The family was doing some last minute shopping. They had split up like a posse agreeing to meet later. She went with Daddy, her sister and brother with Mother. The temperature which her father described as bitter, took on extra meaning when he said it. They were on an important mission: to buy a present for her mother. He took her by the hand, to lead or be led was uncertain.

"Where shall we go? What should we get? Do you have any ideas?" he asked, his eyes afire with possibilities. His mind drawing a blank.

She envisioned the department stores full of luxuries awaiting investigation, Lerner's, Hibbard's, Furr's, (of course they would never go into The Grey Rose.) But, since it was Christmas, there was a possibility they might go to the May Company. She hoped so. It was a modern store with high ceilings and an elevator. She had been there several times before when her parents had saved enough Green Stamps to get a clothes hamper and a set of canisters. She had thought their problems might be solved when she saw all the things you could get with Green Stamps. In time, they could even get a bathroom scale with a fuzzy pink cover on it.

She walked on in the middle of the winds bickering over the Continental Divide, trying to imagine what to get for her mother. She had no idea.

"What should we get? What would she like?" Daddy again posed the questions. An impression of mink coats came to mind. Then she remembered something. A while back her mother had said she wanted something. What had it been? It escaped her.

They walked past Michele's. Any box of chocolates in their window looked like a mink coat to her. They passed the camera shop where Daddy always bought film and lenses, never spending less than an hour debating a purchase. They went by Klausen's Book Store where her brother workedin the stock room. Then abruptly

Daddy nudged her into an unfamiliar doorway. "Let's go in here."

She had no idea where they were and had to look around to orient herself. The store was narrow and filled with shelves. There were no Christmas decorations. She saw a case of pocketknives and tobacco, but no one in her family smoked. She saw greeting cards but it wasn't someone's birthday and no relatives had died lately. She saw some shelves with Kleenex, Band-Aids, and toothpaste on them. She thought there must be some mistake, so she looked back towards the door. Sure enough, it was a drug store, not even a chain operation. She stared at the floor. It was streaked with mud from the melted snow. Her galoshes made her look back up.

"Do you see anything she'd like in here?" Daddy asked.

All she could see was vitamins, and Gelusil which they bought by the case for his ulcer. An old man was buying pipe tobacco. Her father turned her by the elbow, as if she were witnessing an illegal transaction. Then he spotted something.

It was boxed and wrapped in blue cellophane. Like a sailor spotting land he crowed, "Look, over here! This would be great!" She revived momentarily. He was beaming. She felt ashamed for having doubted him.

It was a fairly small package so it wasn't mink. What could be so exciting? Maybe it was…could it possibly be…diamonds? She remembered women were supposed to like diamonds more than their best friend. She'd seen this song and dance number on TV. She couldn't picture her mother wearing diamonds, but maybe she'd just never had the chance before. Maybe if she was given real diamonds she'd stop being so downtrodden and show off a little. Maybe she'd act more like the blonde on TV. Maybe she'd let her daughter stay up till nine o'clock. She couldn't stand the excitement any longer. She had to find out what her father had discovered.

Her father lowered the box and tipped it so she could see. "All the way from France," he murmured. The "diamonds" were three blue bottles, bright blue with silver lids and silver labels that had "Evening in Paris" written in cursive across them. On one corner of the box it read, $12.98 Complete Set, Made in the U.S.

She stared at the blue box. She pictured the Eiffel Tower, the photograph of him in uniform, a cream faced Iowa farm boy in France. She thought of the words he used to try to get her to say at the dinner table, "Merci beaucoup," "Oui, Monsieur," and "S'il vous plait." She thought of how many times he called her mother "Battle-axe." Her eyes stalled, fixated on the bottles.

"Do you think Mommy would like them?" he asked.

She nodded, her eyes falling on some kitchen utensils nearby. Then she remembered what her mother had said she wanted for Christmas. A spatula. She wanted a rubber spatula.

# The Map

I was at that age before maps were friends, before even friends were friends. I had been invited to play at a little girl's house after kindergarten, my first invitation outside of the canyon where we lived. I viewed this invitation with doubt, if not suspicion, wondering why me and not some other little girl was chosen.

Sensing my reticence, the girl's mother doubled her enthusiasm. We would bake little cakes, with real sugar, it would be fun!

Cakes sounded intriguing. Were children allowed to bake at her house? Baking was real to me in a way that playing wasn't. I knew about baking from watching my mother bake pies and hamburger buns every day for our restaurant. In awe I would watch my mother up to her elbows in flour have her way with the dough and a rolling pin. By now I wanted to investigate this invitation.

On the designated day, I followed the girl home after school, my lunch pail clanking against my knees. This much I knew: we were headed the wrong way. I thought of my home as if I didn't have one anymore, my family as if I'd never see them again.

The promised cakes were never baked. There was no flour on my hands. At this my suspicions were somewhat confirmed. My parents were right after all, children were to be seen and not heard, the done-to not the doers.

Most vividly, however, I remember the alarmed tone in the mother's voice when she opened the drapes and looked out the picture window. It was snowing heavily, as it is known to do in the Rocky Mountains. Thick silent whorls of flakes were blanketing everything. It was time for me to go, the mother announced.

She hurried me into my coat. Beginning to foresee the future, I told her I didn't know my way home, to which she responded, "Of course you do! Just go back to the school the way you came, and then you can find your way home from there."

I asked if she would let her little girl walk with me to the school, so I wouldn't get lost.

She said no, it was getting dark, and the snow was coming down too fast. She didn't want her little girl out in weather like that.

I said please. She thought I was just being difficult and disappeared into another room.

When she returned her condition had improved. She placed a small white square of paper on my green wool mitten. "Here!" she said, speaking as one who inspired bestows a gift. "I've drawn you a map!" She pointed to some pencil marks on the square of paper. "Now you can't get lost!"

Before she aimed me out of the garage door into the cold falling whiteness, I remembered to say thank you for the nice time I'd had.

I walked straight ahead, concentrating on taking one soft step after the next. My goal was to get far enough away from her house when I could no longer hold onto the lump in my throat and started crying. I didn't want her to know the map meant nothing to me. I couldn't read. The silent snow kept falling.

# The Cherry Coke

In the fifth grade the greatest thing, the sine qua non, was to go to Music's after school and have a coke. Music's was a drugstore with a soda fountain counter along one shiny mirror-lined wall. The kids would go and hang onto a straw looking bored while sipping and stirring their cokes or, for the romantically inclined, cherry cokes. They would sit on the pedestal stools and swing their legs from side to side or occasionally go for a complete spin.

To my girlfriends who had money to spend and more permissive lifestyles this was daily routine. But I had never been to Music's and knew it only as a fantasy of good times unknown to me. Carbonated beverages were forbidden in my family as we were meant to take seriously my father's threats of holes in our stomachs and rotten teeth for which every coke and Pepsi was personally held accountable. Still, I yearned for the taste of a cherry coke in my mouth.

At that time I had a friend named Justine who lived across from a boy named Don. They were very good friends and I soon became the recipient of some vague questions which were most intriguing. Had I ever been to Music's?

Would I go with somebody, if somebody asked me? Did I like cherry cokes?

This went on for weeks before I entered the paradise gates, saw the shiny mirrors, twisted on the high black vinyl stools, and sipped what was the most ambrosial taste I had ever experienced, the dark deep liquid hiding its sweet cherry surprise. That was the beginning of a great romance, two straws in one glass, face to face with Don laughing.

# Ten

The age of serenity. That was ten. Just me and Linda Dana on our bicycles going on adventures to Monument Valley Park or to the end of Tejon Street. Sublimely engrossed in pedaling down the street.

Or working on our rock collections. Or riding horses at Girl Scout camp. We were both obsessed with horses. Planned to own a horse ranch together when we grew up. Equanimity was our posture.

We were not in the throes of romance. We desired nothing more than the pleasure of our own company. The cliques of Junior High had not yet begun to tear us apart.

We performed circus acts on her rusty backyard swing. Totally absorbed in the daring tricks we were perfecting. We needed no audience. We performed for ourselves appreciating our own mastery.

We wanted for nothing. We had our ponytails and our bicycles for transportation. We were independent. Belonged to no one but ourselves.

# Daddy

My father was very proud of his little fingernail. It grew about half an inch beyond the end of his little finger on his left hand. For one reason or another, all the other nails succumbed to the handicaps of being a taxi driver, a butcher, and a schizophrenic son. But this one finger held promise and spoke of finer origins. He looked at it admiringly from time to time while driving, and ticked it anxiously against his thumbnail when he was getting angry.

I was almost protective of his pride in it. Such a feeble vanity. Something he didn't hide. While other fathers boasted a successful practice in medicine, a hole in one at the country club, a tri-level residence with landscaping, or being wordlessly recognized by the maître de, my father was proud of his pinkie.

I did not encourage his doting by saying, "What a fine nail you have Dad." Or "My, how long it is growing." Truthfully, I was a little nonplussed at what a daughter's proper reaction should be regarding a nail of her father's variety. Too much enthusiasm might be somehow discouraging or cheeky. Too little might seem unappreciative, insensitive. I felt stupid as to the deeper meanings I suspected were implied. My choice was always simple and, for him, always right: smile and be quiet. He never had a clue as to the acrobatics it took to maintain such a state of placidness.

The closest thing to loved I knew was being called "Pumpkin." That was the name my family called me when they weren't making me cry. I was a full moon size five. Years later, I admitted to having laser beam eyes. But Pumpkin was all they cared to see in me then, and all I cared to identify. Being sweet was difficult enough considering my genetic ties.

The children in my family developed certain chronic disorders: violent hiccupping, uncontrollable nose bleeds, a proliferation of warts, allergies. It was an unconscious understanding to alleviate something- something we didn't know existed. It secured a small measure of confidence to be able to name your ailment.

There was probably no one more averse to violence than I, yet no one lived more in the wake of motives for murder.

My dismay at cruelty verged on horror and extended to the smallest living thing. One day I was walking to school behind a little boy who was leaving a trail of green ooze. When I finally caught up with him, the humanitarian treatise which the witnessed slaughter prompted, left him in tears. I said, "How would you like to be a little yellow caterpillar crawling along, minding your own business, and have somebody come along and squish you?"

I was sincere. Even inanimate objects, I felt, needed protecting and ought not to be ridiculed. My stuffed animals were very sensitive to favoritism, and, the perfect democrat, I extended to each an equal nightly kiss, although my vested interest in Elephant, Lambie, and Little Angel was far greater than in dumb dog Buffy, never-named poodle, and Blue Bunny. I even harbored a kind of loathing for the turd-shaped hind end of bulldog Tuffy. But I always concealed it when we were face to face, so he never knew it. Besides, he was an orphan and illegitimate. I felt sorry for him. I lost a couple of friends once defending his rear end from their schoolboy snickering.

The worst thing about violence is that it always hits you somewhere between the pancakes and the pancreas. It surges through the blood like adrenaline, yet often cannot be distilled from timid defensiveness. That is the reason, I think, people do not act to interfere with it. From the furor's point of view, wrath is justified.

The rage my father felt because my sister could not swallow a capsule vitamin, swallowed him. She simply could not get it down, choking and gagging repeatedly, but he persisted. It was for her own good. It was his responsibility that she take her vitamin. Besides, her refusal might be deliberate, an expression of contempt to infuriate and defeat him. He was beside himself, determined to dispense justice. He mashed the vitamin viciously into her pancakes while the breakfast-tabled family witnessed. So close and red-faced to her fear, she could feel the heat of his hate burning through her frozen tears.

Most of the time, during these incidents, the rest of us sat like stone worshippers pewed by a wicked minister as he tried to exhort demons from a frightened innocent… Most of the time… Except when he cornered my sister in the bathroom, and I put my body between her and his iron kicks or when my brother and he went into the alley to fight it out on Christmas, after which we opened our presents ashen-faced.

Gift-giving was always disastrous. My mother didn't wrap packages. She would turn the dishpan over the present. The item underneath matching the wrapping in opulence. The inevitable disappointment led to Special Occasion Dread, a disease only recently recognized as seriously widespread.

My father's delight, however, on occasion was unsurpassed, as the time we hiked up to a coral red stand of aspen trees in the mountains. My father was an avid photographer, and among his favorite things to photograph were red leaves.

We were going on a picnic along Rampart Ridge Road. My father spotted a small cluster of bright red trees among the fields of golden aspen far from the road. We stopped and started hiking over the rocky ground, heading straight for the spot of red leaves on the horizon. When we finally arrived there, we stood in awe at the cherry glow of trees surrounding us. Red everywhere. My father's dream come true, and it was truly beautiful.

# Playground

On the playground, the place for practice, Stanley Traxler said, "Salisbury, you're a real card." For once ready with a comeback I said, "Ace of Spades, I suppose!" He laughed. It was one of the happiest moments of Junior High.

I still remember him, golden boy, compared to the duskier color of Pat, his best friend and my first boyfriend. Stanley probably thought I was too smart and he was too dumb, or I was too tall and he was too short, or he was too rich and I was too poor, but I would have given anything to go to Cotillion and dance close to him like Sissy did, or to the Country Club to swim, or to teepee someone's unlucky but fortunate-to-be-chosen house with him.

The Country Club-people with tans and money. People whose mothers smoked and talked and laughed loudly. Not like my house where all but my father were to be seen and not heard. People whose fathers were doctors, dentists, and told jokes. People who dressed up, drank cocktails, had many friends, and might have a horse.

A horse. Undreamed of dream that possessed me. That's all I wanted every year for Christmas.We could keep it in the garage and feed it grass clippings, I reasoned.

I failed to persuade my parents. No pets were allowed in our house, but I'd moon over any animal who would let me pet it. I'd sit for hours with my grandmother's old collie, Goldie, who would put her head in my lap, a soulful communion between us until I had to be told to go to bed.

One day in the ninth grade, I couldn't stand my petless state any longer. That year I'd been given a room upstairs, with a door that wasn't glass where privacy was possible. At a church bazaar I begged, pleaded, squealed a friend's mother into letting me buy a hamster. "Isn't he darling? Isn't he cute?" I treble-cleffed. My friend Sharon said, in a voice lower than usual, "Yes." I couldn't fathom her lack of enthusiasm. Yet.

Disenchantment began when I was watching him motor over my white ruffley bedspread. He was routing nervously. I was cooing and stroking his head with one finger, when a small black pellet squeezed out his behind which was uncomfortably tailless. Surprised, and somewhat embarrassed, by my shock that he was a rodent, I picked him up apologetically and put him back in his cage.

Being tender-hearted I couldn't tolerate or escape the realization that, in fact, I was keeping a prisoner. And I lay awake nights listening to him frantically, incessantly spin his squeaky hamster wheel, taking it as my due.

One morning the cage was empty. The wheel silent. The hamster was nowhere to be found. He was detected soon after by the dreadful smell that wafted up out of the hot air register. The mystery solved, reeked not of victory but of defeat. I felt like a murderer and spent the next day crying inconsolably at school. My friends thought it was stupid. All this for a mouse? A boy, maybe, but all this for a rat? They were unsympathetic as I tortured myself with guilt. Had I failed to put the clothespin on the door? Had he crept along the wall, found the opening of the air vent, thought, "Freedom!" before plunging to his mousey death? I was disconsolate. My only pet. Dead.

The smell got so bad after a few days I had to move out of my room. My father had tried and failed to retrieve my poor pet by vacuuming the vents. It was the first time he had ever been silent when angry, a silence more angry than the words I was afraid of.

# Green

In order to see green, you must be prepared by certain adverse circumstances, for taken-for-granted green does not reveal itself easily. When it comes to green, most of us know but we do not yet perceive.

Bored with the color of lawns, trees, leaves, we ignore that green is liquid gold, the chemistry of molten growth, not really a color at all, but sunlight held in suspension echoing darkroom activity. This can be readily seen under some conditions, but I caution you not to invoke green glibly. It is, after all, the red bloodline of a leaf, the capture of the sun's wealth, the author of biology.

Before I managed to comprehend green, I stared at a ceiling, immobile, as one year turned to the next. In a hospital room the color of concrete, I played a game of connect-the –dots. The dots were the squeaks of shoes as they approached and receded, announcing a passing cast of walkers. My daily variety, this audible connecting of my four walls and a ceiling to corridors beyond.

First, there was the impertinent click-click of the high-heeled. Obviously they weren't sick. Then there was the unctuous squish-squish of orthopedic nurses' shoes going about their business. Next were the reticent, barely advancing steps of visitors who didn't know what to expect and who might get sick just from the sight of who they visited.Worst of all, there was the interminable scuff-scuff of the man who drooled pushing his wheelchair toward catatonic noon. From time to time, the confident plack-plack of doctors' shoes would confirm that authority was about to enter the room. Finally, gratefully, would appear the apologetic, no nonsense, due-in-the-afternoon-after-school-gets-out shoes of my mother, mysterious in their ability to soothe, debilitating as a reminder of my helplessness. Her too heavy shoes approached regularly hoping to find some sign of improvement in my yellow bedrest feet.

It was during this period of a long accounting of shoes by their squeaks that I unwittingly came to see green. It was after my yellow heels had turned towards a more healthy pink, after I had progressed out of the room and down the corridor with my feet in their own pair of shoes.

It was on a day when I found myself in the front yard, open-eyed to witness an expose of leaves, trees, grass blades. It was then that I saw it. Green as complete. Green as transfusion. Green as spring's agent. Green as fluid labor, circulating, storing, transforming, rising up, reaching out, pulling down, converting the usable. Green as life's herald. Green as earth's private nurse. Green as in sun's service. Green as in my youth.

# High School

This is a story about High School and how I went there and got my heart broke when I was a sophomore by a senior. He was a swimmer, and I was probably a better one. But he made me so I couldn't think about English anymore, after all those years, and I hadn't botched it once. How could I sit and listen to Clifton Fadiman when my pants were on fire for Jim Fletemeyer?

Much of the time was boring to a degree that it raised hope when President Kennedy was shot. Only because there was nothing happening. Then at least there was something to grieve and worry about. Here was surely a tragedy which injected remorse and feeling temporarily back into existence.

Envy occupied some of the rest of my time. I wished I had a nineteen-inch waist like Scarlet O'Hara. I wished I was a cheerleader, but my only claim to fame in my family was that I was quiet as a mouse. I wished I could eat potato chips at lunch. I looked greedily at people's Nalley packs. My parents were against it, and I was too cooperative to be diffident. Besides, I didn't have a dime I didn't save to spend on my Mother's birthday present or Christmas.

I had a teacher named Mrs. Chin. I watched her like a hawk. I loved her delicate frame, the soft breasts I glimpsed, the snow white skin somehow repugnant, and the quiet, lithesome French. She had a knowing, shy smile, and to my horror, carried a man's briefcase. I was curious. Nobody but a square would carry a briefcase!

By then certain things were starting to impress me. Things like passion, loneliness, and fantasy. The queer marriages that make up reality: Mrs. Chin and her briefcase, white skin and its divine and repugnant qualities. She told me about a book in which were written, she said this smiling, worldly things. It was then I decided to major in French.

The French lab had Plexiglas partitions. I could see my reflection with the headphones. It was I at the United Nations calming the French ambassadors. Then we moved to Tacoma.

My next French teacher was a slippery, limp-wristed man who lived with his mother and I felt sorry for. He used to get very snippety with the class when he was angry and would quip, "Repetez!" indefinitely. He picked up his feet when he walked like a pony. When I went back to visit after I graduated, he pretended he didn't know me.

Then came Madame Rossignol who was a hick. I didn't see how you could be a hick in French, but she was it. She had a strange shape, almost flat on the top and about 66-inch hips. She wore her dresses above the knees to signify she was still interested in sex and smiled a lot in encouragement but only to the dummies in class. I didn't learn a thing that year.

I didn't used to sit and wish I was dead. It took me to college before I got into that. But in high school I used to feel kind of black until I got mad, and then my hands would shake. But I hardly ever lashed back except once at Marianne Albertson.

Marianne was the kind of "brain" everybody hated. I was always smart, but I knew about other things like the hots, chocolate chips, and the dog races. My mother had remarried and moved us from Colorado Springs when I was sixteen to Tacoma where the slugs swing. I loved Colorado. Tacoma stunk because of the paper mills.

My stepfather brought flowers to the house for his dead wife's picture instead of to my mother. He said I was lucky to be somewhere it was green. I thought it would be nice to be somewhere I could breathe! I complained about the rain until I hoped he would send me back. But my father would have probably tried to kidnap me and that would have been hard to explain to the cops. I had no choice but to stay put.

One Sunday we went on a picnic. My sister exclaimed, "Hey Louise, somebody dropped their dill pickles!" I didn't have to taste them to know they weren't kosher. Since when did pickles crawl slowly?

One Thursday in November, I stayed after school to fold programs for the football game. Marianne Albertson (not Marianne Faithful who made me want to undress in the wind when she sang in that see-through English voice of hers) found out I was from Colorado Springs. She had lived there one year as her father was a professor at Colorado College, three blocks from where we lived, whose campus I had walked across alone at night blessing each step and scared of the next.

Marianne kept going on and on about the "communist" newspaper, "The Gazette Telegraph", as threateningly communist as plum pudding. Marianne, on the podium, shrieked on and on as the folders folded, I among them. I thought of the newspaper which laid on our porch every morning. Which my brother had delivered, bags bulging, on his bike. And which my sister and I helped fold on Sundays, or helped pull the wagon when we were snowed in or when Glenn went to camp.

Sincerely, I had no idea what she meant by communist, since all I read was the comics, and all I thought about communism was that if Khrushchev were dead the world would be a better place to live in. But I was mad and internally wanted to put an end to Marianne. I didn't make a big deal of it when I was mad, as I said, my hands just shook. But my hate could have been bottled like extract and sat there right next to the vanilla. I put down my programs quietly and deliberately and left.

I knew I was different because I wore black tights. Everyone else wore bobby socks or nylons. I was a beatnik, inside, high-class depression. I was in a coffee house called "Le Chat Noir" if you were a sophisticate, "The Black Cat" if you were plebian.

This girl was a folksinger and sang about how it was dark as a dungeon way down in the mines. She probably went home and watched "Donna Reed" just like me, but I was happy just to sit there listening and be melancholy.

A hood kissed me once. I couldn't believe it! He smoked and sassed the principal. I hoped he would do more, but he didn't. I don't think he knew I existed. His lips were just overly solicitous.

One night there was an MYF party. A luau- no sun or ocean for thousands of miles-but someone would bring canned pineapple chunks and someone would wear a muumuu and thongs. I came downstairs feeling frisky. The hood would be there. My mother took one look at me and in her I'll-do-you-murder tone of voice said, "You can't wear that!" There was one inch of midriff "exposed" as she said. Same as the policeman had said in the principal's office in the sixth grade when they made us tell what we had seen a man do in the underpass.

The underpass was a highpoint in those days. I was especially intrigued by one piece of graffiti in which the artist had scientifically labelled all the parts… boobs, tits, fuzz…" Unfortunately the information was never explicit enough for me and I lived to the ripe old age of eight believing my mother would never even undress in front of my father.

Getting back to the subject of my being "exposed." My mother won, as the person who has the car keys always does when you want to go somewhere. And I came back downstairs in my pink blouse with the Peter Pan collar buttoned telling myself it was somehow better this way. Safe from rapists and would-be rapists, but assuredly never to get another of Jerry Kraetle's cast-off kisses.

I never did major in French.

# Maternity

The first time, I took a rug I was making to the hospital. No one had told me.

The second time, no one had to tell me not to bother with handwork during delivery.

What they never told me, which is almost everything, is that you will never be the same. Never again will you come and go freely. From then on , every absence will create a consequent regret to which return becomes of critical urgency.

What they don't tell you is that you will look down between your legs and see the sac of your femininity hanging down around your knees, and, horrified, you will decide, " What the heck?"

What they don't tell you is that nursing will be among your most erotic bonds.

What they don't tell you is that the smell of your baby's utterly soft head will be the most powerful aphrodisiac you will ever get.

What they don't tell you is that after recognizing your closest kin in the unflinching, pensive eyes of your children, you would and you will do anything for them, including die or not die, harder yet.

What they don't tell you is that fathers take a sentimental, virile pride in their offspring, which (after the earthquake within) you are liable to mistake for mutual comprehension. Women always overestimate their men.

# Shaft

   She was seated swiftly by his latest of
eight wives whose smile was so practiced it
never receded. She tried to focus on the
surroundings of this ironically named living
room, tried to make the setting more real than
her stomach's lining. The clutter of chairs,
end tables, lamps made an impression of
capture. Each chair stuffed but somehow
straight-backed was presided over by an
Eisenhower lamp. The too bright light of
inquisition aimed at her unadaptable hands. The
chair was covered in a rust and brown weave
topped with plastic to keep it from wearing
out, though there was little danger of that. No
one would choose to remain seated in that room.

      The walls were covered with his picture
frames, frames constructed on the same circular
saw that had almost cut his thumb off thirty
years ago. The frames were exactly the same,
varnished brightly, then glued with adamancy at
the four corners, encasing almost identical
scenic shots from Arizona Highways or from
Realities, a religious glossy that featured
Easter lilies close-up.Where wall space had run

out, the pictures sat framed in stacks next to the baseboards.

She listened to him whistling in the bathroom, whistling that came in sporadic jabs, notes that tweetered and festered and then fell off without conclusion. Then there was silence, which was not lacking in impact, then starting up again for no reason with more stabs at a tune making a mockery of rhythm, then sinking back into a prolonged yet inventoried oblivion.

She could picture his broad,high forehead turning red as he looked in the mirror, readying himself to face her after twenty years, his jaw working like a piston, his neck rigged with veins, his temples erect, his eyes intense.  Suave in the mirror, his manicure was nearly complete, his whistling to indicate composure, his thinness to indicate need.

She remembered the time he had dropped the rock down the abandoned mine shaft at Cripple Creek. He had called her over to demonstrate. A good daughter, she had complied reluctantly but immediately. Picking up the biggest rock he could lift, he lined it up deliberately, directly over the black hole of the mine shaft. He paused, then opened his fingers. The rock plummeted without a sound. He did not move a muscle, and she was afraid to. She imagined people standing below, crushed, wounded critically by the falling rock whose speed was accumulating, accelerating as she stood there frozen. The sound of their screams failed to materialize to drown out the sound of the rock that never stopped falling. She wasn't sure what to take as a cue to end this exercise in listening, so she did what she always did, and waited for him, waited till he grinned as if they had done something together. Forbidden.

Eventually the spasmodic whistling stopped. After a sufficiently long time had passed, to eliminate any pretext of consideration, he appeared in the living room. His slack body seemed to recede under his forward neck. He did not glance right or left to acknowledge the other four faces who sat in chaired suspension anticipating his entrance.He did not sit down. He did not advance. He did not clear his throat. He studied her from a distance without emotion or interest.

Finally, he jabbed the keys and loose change in his pocket with the knuckle of his thumb. He looked at her steadily, lined her up carefully as a rock over a bottomless mine shaft, and asked, "What's your name?"

# The Boarders

I was divorced, working at a job as a cook for $4.40 an hour. A single mother with a teenage son and a toddler daughter. I was selling my clothes at a consignment shop to get money to buy groceries. The clerk there was chatty and helpful. She asked why I was selling my clothes, and I told her the real reason. I needed groceries more than clothes. She asked if I lived in a house and, if so, if it had any extra bedrooms. I answered yes and yes. Then she said the magic words, "You should take in boarders."

She gave me a card with the name of an organization that placed foreign exchange students. I went home and set to work opening a chapter of my life that would last 11 years and involve 35 foreign exchange students from Japan, Thailand, Taiwan, Switzerland, and Russia. This chapter would end with my own son going to college in Tokyo and opening his own company where he has been for the past 27 years. But I'm getting ahead of myself. Back to the boarders.

First there was Yuto. He was a happy go lucky nineteen year old who loved to drive his friends around in his car, who I never saw study, and who had the grades to prove it. "No problem" was Yuto's favorite English phrase and I was happy to hear it until the morning our dog, Fritz, ate his contact lenses. I was mortified, took him to the eye doctor and bought him new ones, saying over and over, "I'm so sorry, Yuto." But it wasn't enough.

One night while we were watching TV, Yuto quietly took out his cigarette lighter and lit Fritz's tail on fire. The shocked dog looked at me in horror. Yuto had taken his revenge.

Then came Kosuke, a serious, hardworking social worker working on his P.H.D. Kosuke never said, "No problem," or drove around in a car laughing with his friends. He studied and studied hard for six years.Then he married a petit, sophisticated Japanese bride and finally smiled on his wedding day. But wait, I have photos of Kosuke dancing with my daughter in the living room, so he must have had some fun outside of reading the huge books he always carried home. His seriousness served him well, however. He is a professor of Social Work in Japan now and highly respected.

Ah Kum was a quiet girl from Taiwan. She was an art student and had a dedication that I admired. Her English was deplorable and it was a challenge proof reading her papers. She was frugal, using a bar of soap down to the last molecule and wearing the same sweatshirt and sweatpants for months at a time.

I spent a year teaching English at a Kindergarten in her hometown of Taichung in 2001, where the children were darling and the teachers were in love with them.

Taisei had a big appetite. One night I made chicken curry. There were 12 thighs laid out on a platter. I had two and Taisei ate nine before my daughter could get to the table. When she got to the table and looked at the nearly empty platter, she burst into tears. "What about me," she cried.

Then came more girls, two or three at a time. All demure, sweet, considerate Japanese girls who brushed my daughter's long hair and gave her their old dresses to wear except for Yuna. Yuna was boy crazy and manipulated men with a skill that would make a professional blush. One day she drove home in a brand new shiny red Toyota that her boyfriend of the moment, George, had bought her.

Shortly after using George to get her a new car, she got intrigued by another boy who had the temerityto slap her during an argument. "I thought I was dead," she confessed to me. It didn't stop her though. Her plethora of romantic escapadescontinued unabated after she returned to Japan. Her roommates would discuss it in shocking detail amongst themselves. She was classic femme fatale.

Misaki and Takumi were the family angels. A married couple, they lived downstairs and barbequed in the backyard welcoming everyone in the house. Misaki was shy and sweet and always apologizing for her bad English. She was like a steadfast playmate to my daughter. She gave me her prize kimono on my 36th birthday. Takumi hung Christmas lights around our windows. They gave me their grandmother's favorite Japanese doll as well as beautiful calligraphy scrolls written by Takumi's father.

Later, Takumi's father would help my son get accepted in Sophia University in Tokyo, and Takumi would go on to work in my son's company.

Dang came from Thailand. He was quiet and kept to himself about why he had been kicked out of his previous homestay. I soon found out why. He called me from jail one day asking for me to come pick him up, saying he was confused.

He had been arrested for shoplifting which wasn't necessary because his family was very wealthy sending his friends intercontinental airline tickets to come to an impromptu party for Dang.

According to Dang, "A big black man ran up to me and told me to hold this bag. I am very confused." Always willing to give the benefit of the doubt, I called the Department store detective and asked if that could be true. He said, "No way. We have to see them take something, see them conceal it on their person, and see them leave the store with it before we can arrest them."

After further inquiries I found out Dang had been kicked out of his previous homestay for stealing from the other occupants. I had to ask Dang to leave. Very delicately I handled his fragile ego fearing retribution. Oddly enough, he wrote me a lucid, sincere letter after a few months had passed, apologizing for his behavior in my house. Thus I developed a soft spot for a thief.

Then came Bridget from Switzerland. She refused to eat the food I cooked. She gained all her nutritional needs from a packet of white rolls eaten with honey and a whole watermelon. She would cut the top off the watermelon, put it between her knees, and eat it with a spoon in front of the TV. One night she saw a commercial about a burglar on TV, and she became afraid. She ordered a gun. When I found the gun and told her I didn't want guns in my house, she called her Daddy in Switzerland. He wired her money to move out of my house the next day.

After that she went on a trip around the world seeming to overcome her fear rather suddenly. She sent me photos documenting her travels: Bridget in China, Bridget in Saudi Arabia, Bridget in Ecuador, Bridget in Africa. I wondered if she was finding watermelon in all those places.

But the saga of Bridget paled in comparison to my Russian exchange student, Alena. Alena and Thurman were a package deal. Alena was eighteen and Thurman was a forty-five year old American. Thurman's face was disfigured which gave him a distinctive character. He was also very intelligent and I enjoyed repartee with him until he started telling me stories about the Mexican mafia coming after him.

Alena was on a student visa, but she refused to go to school. She was too smart for it, she said. She felt superior to everyone with the exception, perhaps, of Thurman who had been her ESL teacher in Russia.

They drove around in a noisy dilapidated VW bug without a muffler, and I always knew when they were coming.

Alena was hostile to my daughter, criticizing how she kept her room, and barging in on her in the middle of the night to use her telephone. For these intrusions she would never apologize or tiptoe quietly, but she would act as if she was entitled to my daughter's room anytime she felt like it. We called her Queen Alena.

Thurman and Alena needed money and every night I would overhear long debates about how to get it. That's when the proposal to import Mexican lumber was introduced. The only problem was that it was illegal, and Thurman didn't want to do business with the Mexican mafia. The next night it would be another scheme with a similar drawback of bringing the Russian mob into the picture. I had had enough. I was trying to provide a safe, loving home for my children and the words "mafia" and "mob" didn't figure into it.

At the same time they discussed their criminal schemes for making money, they stopped paying any rent. They told me they were leaving in two weeks. I could handle that. But the two weeks would come and go and there they still were. Then they would say in another two weeks they would move. This went on for months. Thurman and Alena were my undoing. I decided to sell the house and downsize, so I wouldn't have the onerous task of throwing people out who didn't pay rent.

I sold the house eventually, but the charmed Japanese connection had been made. Like-minded Yumiko who had been a dancer, Sakura who was sweet and big-sisterly, Kota who wore wild orange and green printed suits, Harato whose shyness was legendary remain dear to my heart.

I cooked big family dinners every night. We roller skated in a big circle  through the house  starting in the kitchen, going through the dining room, then through the living room, on to the hallway, and back to the kitchen again. We watched fireworks on the roof and ate osechi on New Years. We danced unreservedly and dressed up in my old dance costumes for Halloween. We had a good time.

My son became enamored of all things Japanese, the girls, the language, the art, the traditions, the relatives. He decided to go to college in Tokyo. With Takumi's father's help he was accepted at Sophia University and got into WakeiJuku, an infamous dormitory in Tokyo. He graduated with honors. After graduation he worked at Pan Nations Consulting until he opened his own business training Japanese businessmen to do cross cultural business. He married his Japanese sweetheart and had three beautiful children.

Takumi works for my son travelling from Osaka to Tokyo every week.

I went on to teach English in Japan for five years as well, living near Kyoto. The land and its people are truly charmed, and we were blessed to share our lives with them. All this was due to having boarders.

# The Body

The body is a sullen spouse, a toddler who becomes immobile when you're in a hurry. The body is a constant footnote interrupting the flow of reading. Our intellectual predispositions are not allowed to travel unfettered. As I write, a ragged fingernail holds the pen, shaming me. I know I will have to do something about it, for it has begun calling me names. "Orphan Annie." Unkempt Kindergartner." "Cuticle Abuser." Finally, I will have to put down my pen, paw through my purse like a groundhog, and find the emery board to smooth out the ragged calcium. I don't appreciate interruptions like this, and my fingernails know it. They beg my pardon with their humble stubbiness, but it is not their fault.

I treat my hands with negligence. I garden, dig in the dirt with them as if they were trowels or rakes until the nails are clotted black, and the hands are covered with bloody scratches from rose thorns. People look at me astonished, as if I am stupid, and say, "Don't you wear GLOVES?" But it doesn't occur to me.

I ignore the body's requests for coddling until I am confronted with an uprising of Bastille proportions. An ulcer, a migraine, a back that won't straighten, five night's without sleep, a cough that bleeds. You'd think I would learn, but I am stubborn.

I am afraid to let the body dictate, for the body lives to sleep and eat. Even those who demand rigorous performance from the body know the body longs only to submerge itself in food, drink, sleep, and now and then a good petting. These are the ambitions of my dog. The body doesn't imagine there are better things to do, and perhaps there aren't.

But what about the mind's myriad constructs? What about the ambitious intellect? The mind is unimpressed with primordial goals-to sleep unaroused, to eat to contentment, to grow in any direction. Likewise, the body is not impressed with mental gymnastics, the elaborate architecture of plans, the aerobic maintenance programs. It is a stand-off. A marriage for life, past romance, requiring diplomatic relations on both sides. Compromises are struck, deals made, bargains are exacted, like this one:

Mind (mediating): If you'll just get me through this ballet class, I'll let you have a latte afterwards.

Body (sulking): It's not enough. This barre has really been a killer. My leg has been sticking straight up by my ear for an hour now. My thighs are aching. I deserve a brownie.

Mind (calculating): A brownie, huh? I don't know… it's fattening. But maybe if I give in she'll perk up. If she's in a better mood she won't put up such a fuss when I try to talk her into taking the dog for a walk this afternoon. I've been feeling really guilty about the dog lately. Ok, you can have a latte and a brownie.

Body (relieved): Thanks.

Mind (boldly): Now get your leg up. Class isn't over yet.

Body (muttering): Slave driver.

The mind is pleased, thinking it has once again maintained the upper hand. But the body is no fool. It knows there are countries with siestas after lunch, where Sangria is poured throughout the evening, where pasta is a staple, where dinner lasts until 10:00, when music lulls you back to sleep again. And the body intends to do something about it.

Tonight it will conjure up dreams of Spain, Mexico, Italy, and the mind will awaken wanting to vacation. Then, thinking itself efficacious, the mind will propose, "Why don't we just take it easy today?"

Inside, the body will smile, as if gracefully giving way. "Whatever you say."

# The Gift

What was it Bobo had said when she asked him what he thought about death? Bobo, that old soul, that wise child nearly a man, swept by a tidal wave from cliffs. Swept by power into stillness. Away from a mother's grasp into retrospect. Away from the moment of stunning. Bobo, her son, taken by the tide. Served up by the sea like an oyster, identifiable by the belt buckle only.

What was it he had said before the wave columned? That life was like an overcoat to be shed. That we go on to other lessons. Where had he gotten that, she wondered, not recognizing her own education. What thoughts for a kid, that unnerving scholarliness of his.

She had felt jilted like a lover when they laid him away. Until that night when he came to her in a dream, teasing her from behind her grandfather's spectacles, playing a child's game of hide and seek. "Now you see me, now you don't," he posed, as if life had been in sport. His head kept popping up, eyes gleaming, playing the game of ancestry…Grandfather, Mother… Me. The trick of donning personalities.

At first she had been peeved. He was trifling with her, wasn't he? Poking out first from behind her, then to one side, then in front of her, winking. Appearing first as grandpa, then Bobo, then a mixture of the two.

The eyes twinkling with the secret ingredient, the ingredient that had been missing from the body washed up days before. She had wanted to defend her grief but gradually felt compelled to see the humor in it. The fragile old spectacles being peered through by the callow eyes of youth. Her serious son playing the clown for her benefit. The eyes of one generation impersonating the next, impersonating the next. The lens the same, the vantage point different.

Solveig awoke from the dream glowing, as if her insides were visible. To the hollow of her heart an inviolable gift had been delivered. The oyster had given up its pearl.

# A Dancer's Final Bow

For thirty years she had been a dancer. All that she loved had taken place on a polished hardwood floor and was reflected in a wall of shiny mirrors. For thirty years she had danced, performed, taught, and explored the magic of her soul physically.

Now, in the act of taking her cassette player out of the trunk of her car, she would make her final bow.

She was preparing for a student recital in two weeks. She was excited to meet with her Jazz Dance class. She was up to her elbows in making costumes, recording the music, readying her dancers for their next glorious moment onstage, their parents in the audience beaming.

A car in the parking lot backed up, didn't see her taking her cassette player out of the trunk, continued backing into her kneecaps. She screamed.

The driver stepped on the gas pedal with the car in reverse. The car surged backwards. She could do nothing but plie, pinned between the two cars, in her final bow to the pavement.

# The Breakdown

The first thing she noticed was that she couldn't finish a sentence. She would say a few words and the spaces between the words would grow into a yawning abyss. She would fall and flounder in the abyss and by the time she would come up she would have forgotten what she was saying. So she stopped talking, preferring to be left alone with her post it notes on which she would write every fragment of a thought. The post it notes were laid out in her room like a frightening patchwork quilt. They told her what to do, where to go, and when. It was a lot to keep track of.

She had several ideas that grew in her mind like morning glories and could not be rooted out. Her ex was trying to poison her. He had placed ads on the sides of buses and in local newspapers to torment and derogate her. The TV suddenly sprouted twisted evil channels meant to mock her. John F. Kennedy Jr.'s plane hadn't gone down. It was all a hoax. Yes, the TV was definitely talking directly to her. Eye contact was a fixation, a direct line into her soul, even if it was a news anchorman.

She felt compelled to highlight all the newspapers to show evidence of the secret messages being sent to her to her family who didn't believe her. Her highlighted evidence lay all over the house but still they didn't believe.

She would get in her car and forget where she was going. The streets all looked strange to her, so she would get out and walk, walking in circles. Lost.

When lost in Arizona she looked up and saw that the crows knew what they were doing, so she followed them. With complete faith she followed the crows. With complete confidence they led her.

She wanted to preserve everything that was precious to her and keep it safe, so she took her Native American beadwork and put it in a suitcase.She put in her son's long blonde braid tied with a velvet ribbon, her Japanese kimono from Misaki, her Russian hand carved salt set, her Persian necklace from her boyfriend  before they were married, her daughter's blue corduroy unicorn overalls, and her son's superstar pants with the red rhinestone hearts on them. All these treasures she wanted to protect. The treasures of a lifetime. She looked for a safe place. Not in her house where everyone was suspicious of her. She walked outside and saw a huge dumpster. There they would be safe. No one would think of looking there. She heaved the suitcase in. Her treasures safe at last in the garbage.

The paranoia worsened. She thought the people driving in cars behind her were after her. She stopped driving and ran into a fire station. She told the firemen she was being chased, and she needed to go into the witness protection program. The firemen were amused.

She realized they were in on it. She asked if she was under arrest. They said no and looked at each other knowingly. She left.

She walked to a restaurant where the silverware had blue handles. She began to relax. Her best friend Jewel loved blue, wore only blue. Everything blue reminded her of Jewel, her confidant, her safety net, so she left the only remaining thing she had of value, her purse, in the booth next to the blue spoons and went home.

Later that afternoon a policeman came to the door and returned the purse to her. She realized there were still some nice people in the world after all.

She took a walk through the neighborhood and detected that among the secrets she was privy to know about was the presence of a big game. All the neighbors were involved. There were two teams in the game, one having to do with water and one having to do with the color blue. Houses on the water team were sprinkling their lawns, washing their cars, running through the sprinklers with their children. They were doing these things to signify which team they were on. The blue team had all bought cerulean blue cars which they parked in their driveways to show their affiliation to her friend Jewel's team. Naturally, she was a supporter of the blue team.

She read the Bible for comfort. Passages would light up in neon gold for her to take notice of them. There was gold sparkle dust in the air in front of her vision when things were good. When things were bad there was a strong smell of burning rubber and sulphur. With these cues to guide her she could proceed.

On the Rez she followed the gold dust and learned to stay away from the sulphur. She took all her sacred objects and placed them in significant places. The little book of poems and photos she'd made for her husband before they were married, she left on an altar in a church in Chinle. Her statue of Maria she placed above a jewelry store near Lukachukai. Her basket of quilts and turquoise jewelry she took to a Trading Post at Rock Point. She asked the proprietor, "Can I leave these here?" The woman nodded solemnly. The Navajos understood her. When she went back two weeks later, the proprietor returned the basket to her without question. She was forever grateful.

She remembers putting her cat in the car and driving to a Navajo village. Holding an arrow in her hand for protection, she went into a convenience store and asked everyone if they had seen her cat. The people looked like ghosts. Growing more and more confused she got the feeling she was asking the wrong question, so she asked more definitively, "Am I dead?" The man behind the counter said, "No," so she left. Her dear cat was still in the car hiding from her.

Another time she found herself on an airplane, flying to Italy with two Japanese friends. She looked out and saw the clouds piling higher and higher. She shouted, "Segoi," too enthusiastically using her pitifully limited Japanese. Then she closed her eyes and saw the Akashic records scrolling past her eyes. The story of her finite life recorded for infinity looking like the rolling credits at the end of a movie.

She remembers falling to the floor and a stewardess saying, "Can you hear me?" but she couldn't open her eyes. So when they had a layover in Germany an ambulance came and took her somewhere that looked like a hallway in an abandoned building. Her friends decided to take her back to Japan. She had ruined their vacation.

When they got back they called her son in Tokyo to come and get her. When he got there he had to deal with the police on a matter that had occurred at a beauty Salon before she left. She had gotten her hair cut and when the appointment was over the hairdresser held up someone else's purse and asked, "Which one?" He had a curious smile on his face and she thought he was playing a game with her. He held up a credit card and said, "This one?" Playing along with his game, she said, "Yes," and he gave her the receipt to sign along with the stranger's purse which she obediently took home.

Now her son had the onerous task of explaining to two policemen why this crazy American woman shouldn't be arrested for stealing. After much negotiation in flawless Japanese on her son's part she wasn't arrested that night. When, she later wondered, had he learned the Japanese equivalents to delusional and psychotic break?

Her son found her a kind English speaking doctor who complimented her on her English speaking ability. The spaces between the words came together again, and she was left with these memories and the ruins of the consequences.

# The Bugle Boy

He called to tell her he was making progress in playing the bugle, but he was still having trouble hitting the high C's. He was excited because he had been asked to play at an army veteran's funeral. He wanted to do his best, but the bugle is not an easy instrument to play he said. He was an accomplished professional musician and had played music all his life, but she would remember him most fondly for his concerts with his son who had Down's syndrome.

He had had the patience to teach his son who couldn't read to play the recorder, and they would do concerts together at churches and old folks' homes. There was a simple parity and dignity in their playing together, unachievable otherwise. They played beautifully without accolade and by that his sister was truly moved.

One night he was walking home when a car hit and killed him. Never again would his son play the recorder. Never again would he worry about being a good enough Bugle Boy.

# Death Watch

A mother lay dying in the hospital. Her three grown children were by her side. They had been expecting this, after all, she was 93.

She was unconscious. Her breathing was labored. She had requested a D.N.R.* be put in place, so her three children simply waited.

She didn't like the tubes in her arm or the clamp on her index finger, so she tried to pull them out. Her daughter scolded her for it.

It wasn't supposed to be like this. Scolding her instead of telling her what a good mother she had been, sewing the girls' new dresses at Easter, flannel pajamas at Christmas, ironing their clothes hour after hour at night while everyone else was watching TV, baking cinnamon rolls from scratch which Daddy said were worth a million bucks, sewing drapes for J.C. Penney's, visiting her daughter daily in the hospital, teaching first graders to read, always doing for others, always working, working. Her daughter wanted to thank her for all those things but instead she scolded, "Don't do that." It wasn't supposed to be like this.

A nurse rushed in and asserted the treatments that were available to assist her troubled breathing. They explained about the D.N.R. The nurse said, "Oh," pulled the curtain swiftly closed, and left.

It wasn't supposed to be like this. Doing nothing when something could still be done. Her daughter felt her mother's life slipping through her fingers. She felt like she was letting her beautiful mother down, betraying her by waiting, cursing the D.N.R., taking the easy way out, dying, which wasn't , in fact, easy at all.

Her breathing became slower and more desperate. She began opening her mouth wide to try to suck in all the long lost air she could get. It was during one of these great gaping gasps that she died. Mouth and eyes open as if mid scream. Just like the famous painting. It wasn't supposed to be like this. Her face not at peace but frozen in stark alarm. Her children helpless watching.

Her daughter wanted to take her in her arms and say, "I'm sorry, Mommy. I'm so sorry." But instead she covered the awful expression, the silent scream, with the forgiving white sheet.

*D.N.R.- Do not rescusitate

## Closet Me Not

It goes way back- my history in closets. In earliest memory they held a life that was secret, a probable dump for shoes, toys, clothes no longer used. Helpless assets these contents, but the closet itself was a fuse igniting fantasy, mystery, regret, fertility. The silent momentum of time mocked the present.

In the closet I cried for sun suits that defied my toddler size. Hanging to one side, I spied the Garden of Eden sun suits their happiness implied. At two I outgrew the red sandals, but closet bound they reminded, as did the sturdy brown shoes laced firmly up my ankles, I was headed for a place I didn't like the looks of, a place I had every intention of avoiding, a place called grown-up.

In the closet my worst fears were confirmed. A certain sound in my ears pronounced the guilty verdict. The fact that no crime was yet in evidence was mere inconsequence. Given time…I would be found out…convicted absurdly. I believed in my guilt with a conviction Freud would have lauded, but closeted, I also found … truth! The truth of mystery, of singularity, of snowflakes that glow lavender in the dark.

Standing on top of my father's boat like shoes, lurking behind scratchy woolen suits, no one could find me in hide-and-seek. But his closet reeked of starched defeat, closed clothes. "No Options," stated the menswear flatly. I was glad to leave.

Mother's closet was more friendly, storing Christmas ornaments, house-wifey dresses, but an adjustment had to be made for the false premises I detected.

The best closet was anonymous, holding the magic key to permission, garish optimism, a translucent lime green plastic globe with red marbles in it. This globe was success itself, no doubt about it. I had only to hold it, peer into its inner recesses, and the sounds in my ears would be forgotten. Forgiven? Never, but for the time being, forgotten.

Was this heaven? I wasn't sure. But it was better than the too bright kitchen, the too dark bedroom, the too cold living room. The closet had soul, and within it my perceptions keened and grew bold. I addressed friends in fake languages, imagined peeing in front of a crowd, found power in my ability to close a door. For a moment the unfavorable consequences ceased. And I could almost…not quite, but almost…reach the string which pulled on the light switch.

## Other Women

The Idol

The Captain

The Chameleon

The Angel of Mercy

The Bitch

The Empress

The Widow

The Coyote

The Artist

The Gypsy

The Old-Fashioned Girl

The Slut

The Infanta

The Good Girl

The Grandmother

The Madonna

The Runaway

The Sage

# The Idol

She was everything I was not, beautiful,
grown-up, vivacious, engaged. She wore red
lipstick with fingernails to match, high heels,
cinch belts. She sang in a trio for the
soldiers at Fort Carson. She had overcome a
beaklike nose like her father's, a mysterious
man who limped. He never said much, yet didn't
frighten me as other men did. His daughter had
gone beyond her rustic origins of lye soap,
crabapple butter, and church basement suppers.
She had gone on to forbidden states of
animation and elegance.

Her fiancé (I swooned at that word spoken
casually) was overseas. His picture sat framing
his importance. She was my secret romance. I
brushed her back with a hairbrush while she
purred like a cat. I was sure to be Flower Girl
at her wedding, after all, I was the youngest.

She stuck her foot in the bathroom sink to
wash it, an audacious act for a Methodist. As
soon as I was tall enough I would try it, only
to be caught in the act by my father's outraged
cry, "I knew it was coming to this!"

She stood on her head, an impossible feat
as far as I was concerned, and laughed

frequently, another impossible feat. Someday, I vowed, I would be just like her.

Her fiancé returned from Germany. She plucked her eyebrows and said it didn't hurt. I didn't believe her. My mother cut her picture out of the newspaper, feminine, glowing with anticipation. She was a celebrity. "To be wed," it said underneath. I felt like a stranger suddenly.

I was not the Flower Girl at her wedding and could not bring myself to eat the lavender and green mints luring from the reception table's ruffles. The counterfeit Flower Girl ran rudely from table to table chasing the Ring Bearer in his manly little suit with none of the solemnity appropriate to such an occasion. Everyone said they were cute.

Long since, she became the manager of a renowned ice arena. Recently, she visited me on a trip for the World Class Championships for figure skating. Under my humble mother's orders, she looked at my scrapbooks and satisfied herself that I had distinguished myself in my profession as a choreographer. My mother had not been just bragging.

She noticed my grown-up son's eyes and that my daughter of three looks exactly like the girl she used to babysit.

"Nobody knows this," she said under her breath, for the moment looking fifty, "but I have been through beatings." It was not difficult for me to accept, my husband of twenty years having just deserted us.

It was as if a shade was raised that had been between us. Thirty years disappeared in seconds. I was just like her, and she was just like me.

# The Captain

She dressed like a man. She smoked like a man. She drank like a man. She was not a man. She collected sea shells, unobtrusive pebbles, bits of lichen which she could not let lay. She brought them into her cabin. She served her guests mounds of freshly caged crab, pulled, still pinching from the bay, boiled, and buttered on her doorstep. The rest of the time she ran a tight ship.

Her work was the stage, only not the center of it, the backstage, nit and grit, nut and bolt, high and low tech of it. When a ballerina needed an ironing board, it appeared like rudimentary magic. When the Marley had to be laid, she would grab the gaffer's tape. When my soap got locked in the dressing room, she came back the next day jangling her keys from her belt, with a look that reminded it was me, not she, who would forget things. But she didn't really mind, she understood a dancer's wages.

For twenty-three years she'd managed theatres, her latest the Performing Arts Complex of a major university. She would retire soon and was entertaining possibilities, possibilities for the future, a new loft, her own theatre.We went to look at buildings, discussing the pros and cons. With what would a purchase like this be made? I wondered. She lived on her wages. I was curious. Was my salt of the earth friend dreaming? The answer was even more curious. I was matter-of-factly informed she was wealthy, very wealthy. I found it hard to believe, remembering her once ask me, "Who's going to pay for the paper clips?" Not that she was cheap. She had merely taken it upon herself to educate me in the practical, stubborn side of reality. For her, economic display was anathema.

A new proctor was brought to the university, a problem solver. First on the agenda was budget cuts. She was relieved of her position two years prior to her retirement. Instead of a gold watch, she got an infection. Her Old Salt constitution withered to that of an unfeathered baby bird.

I could see a day would come soon when the hospital bed would not be nest enough, and she would have to try out wings she never knew. I kept my mouth shut, but she was mad at my eyesight. To her a soft heart was as bad as a soft head. She abruptly announced that I would have to leave the room, and on my way out I could send Karen in. Her baked potato was waiting. She was not being funny, but what a sense of humor she had.

One night in her office after a performance, she was tired, too tired. So was I. Maybe she was referring to her blind father, whose eyes and son she had been. Maybe she was referring to a life of suspicion and secrecy, being a woman who kept exclusive company with another woman. Maybe she was referring to years spent assisting the narcissists of the theatre world. Maybe she was referring to her failed attempts to thwart injustice with alcohol. Or maybe she just didn't like the concert that evening, for she looked at me and said, "I've seen it all, Louise. I've seen it all."

# The Chameleon

At the time she was a Gibson Girl with a hint of Mimi from La Boheme. She wore her hair haplessly, in a bun, from which delicate tendrils fell, as if she was about to come undone. Her brown eyes were lidded with lethargy and anonymous love. She was hidden away at the barre in the attic of a hermit. She was a classic under an old ballet mistress' thumb. She honed her craft, reproducing style with the subtlety of a con artist. Reproduction would be her calling. Right then, she was working on antiques.

Then she donned a G-string. I wouldn't have recognized the Follies' queen, but her feathered headdress started toppling, and she cursed in a low voice familiar to me. Surprised to see the soulful Mimi, nearly naked on the street on a freezing November eve, she explained that management hadn't paid them for two weeks. They were striking… show biz… Anyway, she tried to look on the bright side, she had some coke backstage.

Her lover was a sensitive, unemployed, Jewish, intellectual divorcee who liked Seattle and the rain. She decided to move to Florida.

Letters arrived. "I've met the most wonderful man. His name's Vito. He's with the mafia. She flew back for a visit. Vito paid for the trip. Her hair was punk, bleached blonde, short on the sides and tall on the top. As she painted her nails, she cracked her gum and complained that Vito kept giving her diamonds as if they were nuthin'. No more Mimi, she was the perfect moll, Bonnie without Clyde. When she got back they were going to visit Vito's brother, Rocky, in the state penn. He was really sweet, she said.

Vito decided to leave his wife, buy a camper, and take her through the sloughs of Florida. I pictured her on a folding chaise lounge next to a fat, balding man beside the RV. "Honey, did you bring the mosquito repellant?" Not surprisingly Vito didn't last long. Surprisingly, he didn't have her bumped off.

At a different address, her new flame was Golda. "But don't tell anyone," she wrote. She's a woman." They were deeply in love. She sent a new picture, punked out in black leather, bare ass to the camera.

The last postmark was from California. She'd clipped an ad for a miracle mail-order wrinkle cream, thinking I needed one. "It works great!" was scrawled across the bottom. All I could think of was the time she told me her mother had charged four fur coats and then burned the house down to collect the insurance. That was in Arizona, before they moved to Oklahoma.

# The Angel of Mercy

Her long white hair was held back in a swirl. She stood alone waiting for the 6:00 A.M. shuttle in front of The Inn At Laredo. Her eyes were the soft grey of amnesty, her size petite, her dignity evident.

We were strangers but fell into the kind of conversation old friends do, who must hurry to catch up with the news. We travelled the distance of fifty years en route from Santa Fe to Albuquerque.

Her husband had just passed away, and it was time to leave New England. She had always wanted to live in Santa Fe, and had come to look for an apartment. To her delight, she found an adobe in the old section.

Had he been sick a long time? I asked. Forty years, so, no, it hadn't been an unexpected death. Looking back, she said, it was as if forty years had been only an instant.

She had fallen in love right out of nursing school. He was daring, romantic, passionate. Then he was drafted… World War II. They got married as a going away present. She was pregnant. After her son was born, she had no place to stay, so she went to the hills and found a farm woman who leased her a shack that used to house chickens. She cleaned it up, made curtains, planted a vegetable garden out back. She lived simply with the sun on her face, in love with her baby. Those years in Kentucky were the best years she said.

One day a telegram appeared. In patriotic fashion the good news was announced first. They were pleased to inform her that her husband would be returning home soon, discharged honorably. His service to his country had been exemplary. The bad news followed, spoken as incongruently as a dog tag dangling a dog. They regretted that her husband had been wounded in action, but he had made considerable progress, and was well enough (and looking forward to) returning home soon. His country was grateful to him.

The man who returned was paraplegic with extensive brain damage as well. He would never speak, write, or walk again. She decided to give him the round the clock care he required herself. Her son resisted, who was this person?

It must have been terribly difficult, I said stupidly. She shot me a look that went back to where it came from almost immediately.

Without a trace of self-pity, but with complete recognition, she answered yes. Then with detectable pride she added, the part of his brain that could do numbers was intact. He could still play poker, so he became a professional. She would accompany him to the games. I imagined this gentle woman wheeling his chair through the smoky din of casinos, past row upon row of jack-handled slots, beyond the roulette wheels, the tables of blackjack, the boards of bingo, and on to the back room deal, the big time games. He must have had a nickname, but it would have been morbid to ask. I could tell by her quiet humor and confidence that his reputation had been formidable.

Before he died she had asked if it would be all right if she sold their home and moved to the Southwest. He'd given his blessing, so here she was breathing sage and pinion.

"When the time comes, I want to show my son the love letters his father wrote me in Kentucky." Quiet for a moment, she said, "He's not quite ready for it yet. You see, he never knew his father… as he was."

# The Bitch

When I first saw her she was playing horse, running across the playground with another little girl, hanging on to her untied sash. The impression was of prancing abandon, but more importantly control over her rider. I watched from the dismal distance of shyness.

She was a liar, cavalier about it, nonsequitor in her uses for the truth. She befriended a new girl by walking her home after school. She claimed her uncle kidnapped little girls, chopped their heads off, and threw them off the top of Pikes Peak. How did she know? She saw the chopped-off heads with ants crawling all over their necks on Sundays when her family went skiing. But, she reassured, if the new girl would be her friend, she would tell her uncle not to do it to her. The new girl was grateful. She said she would be her friend.

Years later, in Junior High, she would get her way with boys by lying. She would get them, get rid of them, get them to get her things, and get them to do or not do things as she required. Her lying seemed to work for her, better than the truth did for me, in much the same way as big breasts did for her mother. Even her daughter tried to button up this woman who was always leaning over. I didn't trust the mother. Didn't trust the bug-eyed dad who drank alcohol till he was red-faced either. Didn't trust the too young aunt who wore big rhinestones on her slippers with her red toenails sticking out. Didn't trust their innuendos about men, or the Hollywood freeway, or fur coats, either. Didn't trust their too-loud laugh about the joke cigarettes their nephew had appeared with. "Horse Shit" cigarettes, the label said. But once or twice this distrust disappeared.

The first time was after the girl had fallen off her bike. I pictured her careening down the steepest hill around, to impress her older brother and his best friend. I imagined her feeling the breeze on her face, until suddenly she tried to brake, then skidding, face down, on the pavement. When I saw her, a week after the accident, she began to cry. It was then that I remembered how beautiful she had been.

The second time was on the playground again, in the only physical fight I had ever been in. I forget what lies had finally prompted me, a quiet, serious student, to stand up to her. I only remember the feeling of pounding my fists into her back between her sharp shoulder blades. It was the feeling that justice was finally being done, and that, being this close to an embrace, I didn't hate her anymore.

# The Empress

She was a shrewd businesswoman. During the Depression, when all about her men with families to support were losing their jobs, she kept hers, clung assiduously like a tick to the back of a department store. Her life consisted of three things: a secret, capitalist enterprise, and her glass collection. All else was interference, annoyance. To pass by her was to shiver. She had the charm of a freestanding ice pick.

The secret, she kept corseted, so no one would know, took a few days off work, and left the secret in a basket at a beauty shop, returning to work thinner, relieved. No one knows why the beauty shop was chosen, or if it was chosen, or if it was just a place to stash the infant. The owners were not of like mind to her. They were a thick, earthy stock given to loud talk, rough living, and drinking. "Throw a rock in China and you'll hit one of my kids,"har, har, the old navy sea captain would brag.

Looking like an old navy sea captain herself, the wife would make no objections, so here the child was raised.

Back at the department store her coworkers asked how her trip had been, wondering if there wasn't something different about her. "Fine," she snapped to shut them up and went back to business. Over the years she climbed with the steely precision of a construction worker on a girder- one false move and you're dancing on air. To dance was out of the question due to her religion, but eventually she became the manager of a chain of department stores. She hired the husbands of her sisters, the husband and father-in-law of the baby she'd left at the beauty shop. She could hire and fire the men of her choosing. She had reached the top.

Time now to devote to her collection. Her house filled with antique glass gave it the appearance of an ice palace. Arranged by color scheme, cranberry glass faded into pink Venetian glass, cornered by Vaseline glass, upstaged by turquoise glass, surrounded by cobalt glass, dazzled by cut crystal, and finally giving in to effusions of flowery Limoges china. The rooms had the look of frozen fireworks, of stalactite draped parlors. She knew the price she'd paid for each item. Even when Parkinson's disease had claimed her, she would pick up a teacup with a hand as agitated as a cement borer's and quote, "$48.95. Limoges."

During the last years of her life she applied herself to the moribund business of not dying with the same disconnected and disconcerting passion with which she had become rich. Her gums succumbed to gangrene before she would go see a dentist. Several times she fell down the stairs, breaking a hip, her back. A succession of strokes kept suggesting perhaps she'd had enough of this life, but she wouldn't hear of it. Her sisters, having cared for the 60 lb. invalid for a decade now, became discouraged. One of them died happily, thinking her sister needed a good example.

Once, when a stroke was thought to be final, the baby left in a beauty shop and her five grown children were summoned. The secret was finally out, but she still didn't die. The oldest grandchild, hoping to detect a familial bond or share in her wisdom, lingered by her bedside. With excruciating difficulty she eked out a few words. The grandchild listened in expectation. Summoning her effort to finish this sentence, she announced, "If I can just hang on till January 12th, I'll get a tax break."

# The Widow

I met her on the picket line, walking the pavement with her sign, a gentle queen, smiling, radiant, glad to be there. Later, I found out why.

She beamed on my little girl, doted like a grandma though she was far too young and far too beautiful for that.

She put on a program for the rest of the school, organizing the bubbly, bony, brown-eyed newcomers to make and do, to put their best foot forward, to act American and strut their stuff, unlike their mothers who stayed at home sewing tedious, articulate needlework depicting tradition and war.

At school the children did handstands and recited Martin Luther King. She had written a poem about Cambodia before the war. Afterwards the gymnasium was silent. She left smiling to herd her brood upstairs. The English As a Second Language program was proud. Today they had been confirmed. Heard. It was Christmas.

I rushed out and bought presents. Feeling cheap and foolish, I handed them out like an embarrassing Santa. It would not have been enough if I had given them my own children.

She called my daughter "Beautiful Rose" and said she reminded her of her youngest. Then she told me about before.

Her husband had put her "above," she said. Her mother told her she must have been very good in a previous life for him to treat her so well. One day her husband took her to the shore. He made her promise she would not marry again until their last child was grown. She did not understand why he said this. She thought he was making a joke. After that they came and took him away. To this day she doesn't know what happened to him.

It disturbs me that I can't remember clearly how many of her children died, or from what, in the refugee camp. But she was pregnant when the remaining ones had to be given to their grandmother, because she was too ill to take care of them.

She lives alone now, in a country where she is one of the lucky ones. Her daughter does not call her "Mother," she says. Long distance calls warn, "It will not go well with you, if you have a lover before the last child is grown."

She speaks little and with many silences. At school she takes good care of children who may forget the pain, know change, perhaps even prosperity. In the halls she is magnanimous, serene, but to me a forward American, blunt with questions, she confesses, "Part of me died."

# The Coyote

She loved her mother, but children were not
for her. Never, no way, no thank you. She ran
rivers. She cut off her braid along with squaw
consciousness, made a detour. Of her heritage
she retained the tradition of living close to
nature, the acquisitions of a nomad, the traits
of a coyote.

At a café over coffee she demonstrated with
the salt and pepper shakers, talked about
respect for the ways of the river, told me how
not to go under. If you start to get sucked in,
don't fight it, don't swim, that's the worst
thing you can do. Get on your back and float
downstream, just go with the river, or it'll
take you.

While I changed diapers, she rode the
Colorado. Between the walls of the Grand Canyon
she took on whitewater, swam naked, drank beer,
and crawled up to caves scrawled on by Anasazi.
The ancient ones approved, revered coyote.

Every few years I'd run into her by chance,
(nothing happens by chance, she would declare.)
We would meet at a used car lot, at a dance
concert, in a field of grass. What had she been

up to? I was always dying to know. She was working with teenage prostitutes, returning from Greece, living in a teepee, working on ski patrol, living out of her car, needing a bath, on her way back to the Grand.

One night she called, had a minute, could she see me? I couldn't that evening, had kids screaming, half a dozen mouths to feed, dishes piling up in the sink, homework from the University clamoring. Call back soon, I begged. Please? Please! She agreed.

I went down the river with her one time, knowing we weren't in the same boat. My children and her freedom haunt me. She may never call again. That's the way with coyotes.

# The Artist

She lived in a loft which is where the magic happened. Every conceivable tool and art supply was contained therein. Her smile was as broad and warm as the sun, as she welcomed me into her universe. I accosted her upon seeing her art in a storefront window. "You are amazing," I said. "Fantastic."

I hung one of her gossamer kimonos with ceramic fish swimming in and out of the obi and a catcher's mask headpiece, likewise with the fish coming and going, in my dance studio, where it presided over my comings and goings like a visionary empress.

She dressed like a punk with short spiky hair, thrift store skirts with cinch belts, cowboy boots painted bright blue, and a dog collar atop numerous chains.

She taught children her wizardry ways, and, after they had an hour of dance at my studio, we would traipse over to hers for art class. A happier bunch of kids you could not find, as they silkscreened, made clay masks and drums, and painted their own costumes for our dance recitals.

She was as generous as she was talented. She made a shiny silver holster filled with colored pens for my son, a budding artist himself. Her ability to accessorize left no stone unturned. She made jewelry from computer chips, necklaces from buttons and paper clips.

She fashioned a Kachina costume for me when I was focusing on Native American imagery, and more kimonos when my husband produced an opera called "Oxymora." Her costumes were extravagant, lush, and always edgy. A geisha with chartreuse hair with arrows going through it. What she would think of next was a tantalizing mystery.

She left Seattle for the big time where she tempted Hollywood with her wares. I was thrilled to see her name flash by while in a movie theatre watching "The Bodyguard" starring Whitney Houston.

Her last letter contained blissful pictures with her own young son, whose smile matched hers watt for watt. I was happy motherhood had not eluded her, as conventional she was not. Her art suspended her above all that, like a kite with papier mache ducks flying through it.

We lost touch. Thirty years passed and I looked her up on the internet. The first thing

I saw was her smiling face next to a ceramic
high heel which turned into a coiled
alligator's tail. Some things never change.

# The Gypsy

Arms akimbo, body pitched forward at an unlikely angle, legs lunging forward as if in jest towards the path ahead, she walked. She was an Irish windmill with an underlying Spanish ferment. She made her way to America telling fortunes on a 747. One look at the cards and she said, "You're spinning, everything's whirling around you." The pilot was impressed. He couldn't deny that, thus, the free trip.

As un-American as a bagpipe she came from a land of open spaces, thatched cottages, rock-piled fences, places where nature hadn't been told to get out and stay out yet. "Hola!" she hailed, and slatternly sauntered towards a new day, as if she wasn't tired of life already. It was that I envied.

Her laughter was ready as unruly hair for a comb, but she made no attempt at composition. Goofy was a term which best described her at basketball. As a Yuppie hellion's nanny, she was sublimely self-assured, even when the four-year-old fired her. His mother wanted to take lessons from her and stayed home one day to see how she did it: how she made Zachary eat his sandwich, how she got Zachary to take his bath, how she got Zachary to release the cat. The mother was desperate, and too intellectual, thinking maybe she could patent the relationship this latest nanny had with her son.

Her name was Carmel and her flavor was butter rum. Wisdom was her prerogative, unsophisticated charm. She was happily indentured as lover to a man with better sense, an American, oddly embarrassed and grateful to have found someone who wasn't like all the rest.

Her gestures were frivolous, her pockets penniless. Her common sense went beyond the repressed. Languorous but not selfish, she waited for an opening in the stiff brittle fabric of American existence, heralding a liberation made aromatic by tradition. She did not joke but had the lightest of humors. Her draped, seemingly strength less lengths of wrist, arm, and neck, impertinently connected to a roundness of hip.

She stalked off, sang off-key with embarrassing abandon, poured over Sangria and Spanish poets, listened to the problems of well-to-do Americans without being

congratulatory. Her effortlessness was beyond
nonchalance.

# The Old-Fashioned Girl

She was born looking backwards. The sights of the modern world were an offense of aesthetics. Used-car lots would disappear if she ignored them. Disdain alone could convince the computer its time had not come.

She chose clothes from closetsful of Victorian rags. The lace of Miss Haversham was at her disposal. Her own family thought her daft, statistically insignificant. As far as she was concerned, they were the ones out of step, in their polyester slacks, trying out new kitchen gadgets.

While video games were creating legions of new addicts, she was tatting. Among the useless things she learned were how to pick up a book gracefully, how to conceal appetites, how never to refuse another's wishes, and Ballet, spelled with a capital.

Her profession was avoiding one, all the while waiting for the world to return to its senses. She was waiting for the skyscraper to whisper, "Just kidding," waiting for one significant thought to surface, to cut through the yuppie metabolic, to humiliate the executive on his two hour lunch break.

Among miracles she hoped for was the transformation of familiar scorn into admiration, for her lover to come back from the marketplace, for mothers to take care of their children, and for the brave to turn back the white man.

# The Slut

People stared. She was used to it. In the
bathroom at school while she ratted her hair up
to there, girls stared. In class, while she put
nail polish on her run, boys stared up her
skirt. On the bus, as she reapplied her blue-
as-a-parrot mascara, passengers couldn't take
their eyes off of her. When she took a rare
communion at church, grandmothers sucked in
their breath, mothers gave thanks their
daughters weren't like her, and the little
girls wondered what she was going to do next.

She was notorious. She thought so what?

At the swimming pool when she got ready to
do her swan dive, random splashing ceased. She
would pause for a moment, as if she were
thoughtful. Then she would practice her
approach-step, step, and jump- to the end of
the board a few times before giving the held-
breaths back to the swimmers. Arching into her
swan dive with her, the voyeurs would come back
to life again. The splashing continued.

Outside she would light up a cigarette,
while everyone else resorted to Reese's peanut
butter cups. She would exhale slowly, leaning
against the white pillars of the YMCA. Way past

dark she would go off with some weight lifter on a motorcycle.

On other nights she could be seen at the Roller Rink, weaving in and out with long sulky strokes, skating backwards when she got bored, barely glancing over her shoulder, turning a quick figure eight to stop instead of just slamming into the wall.

Boys would appear out of nowhere when she undid her laces, older boys who didn't have parents coming to pick them up, boys with cars,not borrowed ones either, but souped-up Chevys with the tops down or off completely.

She would wind a silk scarf around her beehive and tie the ends tight like a choker. Then she would speed off in a convertible, laughing or glaring, whichever suited her.

She had no intention of studying that night.

# The Infanta

For want of a father's love, she took to
her bed. Her mother understood, too well. She
brought her daughter sequins and glue, scissors
and colored paper. Together they set up a
bedside workshop, decorating the room with
their eclectic array of gaily elaborated
decorations. A welfare galaxy housing the
stars, but not the star that mattered- her
father, a famous Hollywood actor. They could
have turned on the TV and seen him parading for
the camera and the audience's laughter, but he
wasn't funny anymore to them.

The mother would go for medicine, doctors,
dieticians. When all else failed, she tried
more imaginative means. Prayer. Meditation.
Scientology. Visualization. Her techniques
became profound. She told me once, she
whispered, she had once gotten a china deer to
shake its head and wink at her, but she
couldn't get her daughter to get up. Her child,
her sweetheart, her dream daughter grew so thin
she didn't rumple the sheets.

Together they invented universes.
Crystalline, fantastical dreams were reality.
The mother would open a ballet studio. The

Infanta would teach belly dancing, her mother Flamenco. Occasionally they would have boyfriends come over and would giggle about them after they'd gone. When they were blue, they would throw a private party, just the two of them. And the Infanta, not being able to digest, and the mother, not wanting to get fat, would spit cake. The mother's merriment was contagious, her beauty arresting, her spirit effervescent. The Infanta was transparent as gauze, ethereal, fatal.

The power of the mother's love was formidably equal to that of the father's absence, and suspended between the opposing forces of these two monoliths, the Infanta sustained and waned… sustained and waned. For twelve years she lay in state until, with faith in Reincarnation, her mother gave her permission to turn her body in and go get a new one. The Infanta was relieved and grateful. As her mother watched in awe, she left her body behind, promptly, with the skill of a magician.

# The Good Girl

She sat pulling the threads one by one out of a long piece of pink gingham. She was making a dress with a border of drawn needlework. It was taking forever, but she was determined to stick to it. No one's patience could outlast hers. She was a good girl.

If it wasn't smocking, it was getting straight A's, blue ribbons at swim meets, perfect attendance at Sunday School, working her way through badges at Girl Scouts, never talking unless she was spoken to, doing without. "By your works, so shall ye be known," didn't it say? And she was known by her works. She was a good girl.

Her silence formed rings around her, as she did her daily devotions. This was not mere quiet time, she had a purpose. Like a pebble tossed into water, her silence emanated outward in waves, trying to push back the sounds of yelling, the daily vomit of hate her father spewed towards her family. In her father's eyes, silence alone made her a good girl. Her accomplishments were in vain, a collection of useless behaviors, as far as he was concerned. For her they were a smoke signal to the outside world. She wasn't finished yet, finished, as in obliterated.

She believed her goodness could save them somehow, if she could just be good enough. But that point never came, so she redoubled her efforts. By example, she would teach her sister to stop sassing back, so her father would stop kicking her. By meekness and subservience she would make up for her mother's stubborn resistance and help her father feel less furious. By contentment she would teach her friends with nicknames like Sissy, Missy, and Bitsy, to appreciate their parents whose harshest words to them were, "You can't talk on the phone longer than forty-five minutes at a time." Maybe if she was good enough, she too would be given a nickname, would be accepted in the club that so eluded her, the club of the casual. If she could just be good enough maybe the fear of the words, "mental illness" would recede, would go away, would, as if by magic, disappear.

So she prayed. She went straight to the top to God with her petition, her plea. She prayed till her ears rang from the pressure inside, at first secretly, pretending she was asleep. Then, thinking perhaps God wasn't listening because she'd omitted the posture, she got on her knees, hands clenched to her forehead. Then she thought maybe her prayers needed more credibility, a sort of a spiritual resume, to back them up, so she read the Bible cover to cover, underlining in red the good parts. Then she thought maybe God considered her a hypocrite for separating her secular life from her religious life, so she prayed while walking to school and went to the sanctuary instead of the cafeteria during lunch.

She continued to be sympathetic to Missy, Bitsy, and Sissy's problems. They had to go to Europe with their parents. It was a long boat ride. They didn't know what to pack.

In the evenings she made her father coffee, just the way he liked it- Sanka with 2 oz. of half and half. He sat in traction with a bag of rocks pulling on his neck drinking his coffee. He couldn't yell while the bag of rocks was pulling against his neck because of the chin strap. That lasted about twenty minutes.

She began to be discouraged. It was hard being this good. She lost friends, confidence, sleep. Why hadn't it helped, all this goodness? She decided to backtrack thinking there must be something wrong.

# The Grandmother

Iowa farm folk, that's what she was. A no-nonsense, hardworking Methodist. The church organist until well into her eighties, her pride and only vanity, except perhaps the pure white corn silk tassel of hair that hung all the way down  the back of her nightie. The rest of the time that baby soft down was coiled at the base of her neck, out of sight, out of mind, as was frivolity.

Her garden expressed the flavor and flourish her personality refused to, and she tended it devotedly with results that those who sat at her table approved. Sweet red tomatoes, even sweeter corn -on-the-cob, homemade pies, jams, pickles, and bread were served on her plates.

The hen house was also her domain, and that of the prowling tomcats. She would scold and threaten when they sucked an egg or captured a chick. A farm was paradise to a tomcat. To her granddaughter, visiting from the mountains of Colorado, the farm was proverbial.

Her house smelled sharply of mildew, rural occupations, outdoor plumbing. It sounded like a train receding in the distance, a crank telephone, a windlass working, a soulful Bessie mooing. It had the feel of patience, persistence, peace.

She had raised five solemn-faced children during the Depression. The youngest had died in the war. The others grew up not to be farmers but kept a formidable respect for hard work and the price of everything. All were college educated and proud, as humble people are, to be so.

I had heard stories of my grandmother storming out of the house and sleeping in the barn sometimes. I couldn't imagine how my strong, silent Grandfather who read books might have provoked these uprisings.

The last time I saw her she sat like a schoolgirl in her fancy clothes. She was on her way to church. Her burgundy dress had been hand sewn, as were all her clothes, and she wore it with a white crocheted collar and a brooch at the neck. My eyes stopped when they reached her feet. Instead of the usual black Dr. Scholl's lace-up pumps, she was wearing a brand new pair of navy blue sneakers, as out of place as landing gear on her defiant feet.

# The Madonna

Contentment is hard to come by. The only contented woman I've ever known was Faith. Faith could have been the model for all of Mary Cassatt's gentle, loving mothers. Peace, serenity, and radiance converged in her features like the Madonna.

One of my numerous jobs as a single mom was housekeeping for Faith. Twelve hours a week I would clean, nonstop aerobic cleaning, which had a hopeless edge to it, for Faith had four children under the age of five. By the time I'd finished scouring, scrubbing, vacuuming, washing, ironing, and tidying up, the house would look exactly as it had when I'd arrived… totally trashed. I'd act like I didn't notice, which seemed like the contented thing to do.

I observed Faith as one might the Milky Way or the Northern Lights, something rare, distant, and extraordinary. Her contentment never varied. She was gently encouraging, infinitely patient, mildly good humored, and serenely grateful at all times. Not for a moment did I doubt her sincerity.

What I couldn't understand, however, was how her kindness and equanimity was startlingly eclipsed by her boys tormenting each other every time she left the room for her quiet time. I can still see the five-year-old trying to choke the three-year-old, banging his head up and down with his hands around his brother's neck, as their mother read the Bible in her bedroom. I can still see the three-year-old purposefully yanking the rocking horse out from under the twin toddlers while they tried to mount it, and the slow Jack Nicholson grin that spread across his face when they fell down on top of each other, bawling. I can still see the toddlers waiting silently until I had folded and put away five loads of laundry before going resolutely over to the cupboard doors, opening them one by one, and methodically pulling out all the clean, folded clothes, then eyeing me steadily to see what my response was going to be. More contentment?

Before long it occurred to me that contentment might merely be a symptom of something, something less than flattering, like landslide denial. Or worse, that it might be a prerequisite for trouble, as in the inextricablylinked dynamics of sado-masochism.

Had Faith been crabbier it might have been more beneficial, safer for the children, less dangerous to the community.

# The Runaway

She harbored darkness. It was her only
hope, to take on the coloring of those she
deferred to. Until she stuck out her thumb,
looking for a way, away from where she'd been.
It was a long time coming. She had no idea
where she was headed. It was two years and, as
yet, there was no indication she had not made a
mistake, but she was determined to correct the
error of his ways.

"You look great," an acquaintance would say
when you wear oblivion well was meant. It was a
vain form of revenge, trying not to appear
manacled. But cheer was not as easily
intimated, and she had given up that expression
long ago. Having nothing but posture at her
disposal, she settled for appearing blankly
proud, a compromise she detested.

But it was softness she craved, softness
she aspired towards vaguely, like the
unexpected found. The grassy hiding place of a
fawn curled round in protection, formed to the
rump, the delicate legs and feet tucked in, the
body warmth still laying claim to its source

already gone. Inebriated, she hunted, held her breath for, stalked softness.

Or its opposite, spontaneity. On terrain that could not be counted on, flirting sprint like spontaneity could get you across. In the absence of faith, impulse could be useful. "Spontaneity," she prayed, marching through her frown. "Softness," she breathed, determined to find a blessing under her stuck up chin.

She wondered how she had lived on his doled out bits of love. Bits so childishly precious they could break her heart, so few and far apart, they did. Still, it had been he who left. She would have endured anything for that moment of forgiveness, a single undoing confusion of caresses.

Now she had to endure the encouragement of her friends. "You are so strong…strong…strong…" they echoed. She wept. She did not want to hear those words ever again. Strength had never been what she intended, brute, boring, and unaligned. She had wanted love. Romance. Almost killed herself for romance.

Now she just wanted an end, an end to a quest that had become absurd. For rest. And for words that didn't hurt, words that didn't press into her flesh like unwanted pairings in a bed.

Words that didn't seduce and curse…seduce and curse… seduce and curse.

So she read, binge reading, done in secret late at night while everyone slept. Feverish. Excessive. Prying at insight. Trying to touch bottom while keeping her head up. Treading water, barely. Bulimic reading, but there was salve in it. Words cooled in print, didn't swell like a bloodthirsty tick. With words she could travel like he'd promised. She could run away.

She would find a cave, cool and damp, smelling of growth and earth, dark, soft, fertile. Smelling of a mother, person of granite, common, constant, firm. Not leaving in succession, not swelling up and dumping like a raucous, receding wave. She would find her way to a cave, to be held by the hollow of rock. She would turn herself into a cave. These were the vows of a runaway.

# The Sage

She had the camouflage of a ptarmigan dressed for winter, a timberline inhabitant's sharp eyes, quick heartbeat, and cautious feet. Like an animal of the tundra she belonged to her setting. Never donning and discarding disguises but blending, as if to pay the environment a compliment.

These days she loves to sit and let her thoughts drift, spinning an invisible thread from corner to corner like a spider. She had had enough of intellectual gymnastics prior to her eightieth birthday. She had earned her equilibrium. She approved the poise of widowhood. She could afford not to be a spendthrift with actions, words, emotions.

It all came down to this. Her two feet side by side on the rug. Her lap disappearing over time. Her children grown and strong. Her sense of line. Her tradition born of Norway. Her abandon encountered in Chicago. Her passion drowned with her son. Her two feet, now turning a pirouette of tranquility, like Ulanova performing an ecstatic retreat.

Vignettes:

Innocence

Discouraged

A Chance

Regret

Anger

Things My Parents Made Me Do

Girlfriends

Jobs

Color

Clothing

Courage

Denouement

Gifts

Time

Music

# Innocence

It was a Saturday morning. I was five, my sister was seven, my brother ten. We had paid our two milk bottle tops apiece to get into the movie theatre for the Kiddie Show featuring Roy Rogers and Trigger. My brother headed upstairs for the balcony. My sister and I sat down in the dark on the main floor. A man sat down next to my sister. The movie had started when my sister whispered to me that we had to leave. Annoyed that we had to go I asked, "Why?" She told me the man had put his hand on her leg. She was innocent.

A year later I was feeling like a failure, because I couldn't ride the big kids' bikes like my brother and sister. Then one glorious afternoon I was at a friend's house when I discovered I could easily ride a small bike that was proportionate to my height. As I flew down the sidewalk on the little blue bike without wobbling, I was exhilarated. Released from the shame of having failed, I was innocent.

As a girl of ten I answered the phone one night when a low furtive voice said slowly, "Can I tongue you?" Maligned and horrified I slammed the phone down. I didn't know what the words meant. Only that it was ominous. I was innocent.

In the ninth grade I was at a school dance slow dancing with a boy who had a hard-on. I was appalled and moved away from him. I never spoke to him again. I was innocent.

In high school at my first ballet class I was informed by a snooty ballerina not to wear underpants under my tights. "No one wears underpants," she sneered. I was grateful she told me. I didn't know. I was innocent.

Beginners at anything are innocents and should be treated delicately. My watercolor teacher at the first lesson commanded, "Show me your brushes!" I pulled out six fluffy brushes which came in a set. Taken aback she said, "Never buy brushes in a set. Throw these away or give them to some children. Brushes should come to a point." And she demonstrated this fact with her own beautifully articulated brushes. I had no idea. I was innocent.

In college I was a cocktail waitress at a Greek restaurant where Greek sailors came to watch Medea, the belly dancer. Never having had a drink in my life, I was ignorant of people who indulged their vices. I hesitated to serve customers more than two drinks, not wanting them to get drunk. One night when the owner, Maria, picked up the cash register and threw it at her red-faced alcoholic husband who was yelling at her, I was surprised. I was innocent.

My husband and I were strolling in Seattle Center one Sunday afternoon. Two ten-year-old Native American boys were fighting on the grass. My two-year-old son walked up to them and patted one of the boys who was crying on the back saying, "Okay?" The boys stopped fighting. My husband and I had tears in our eyes. Our son was innocent.

Later at eight when my son tried to control his facial expressions, he would become "Mr. Serious" at will. He tried to give me "Mr. Serious lessons" and would arrange my features into an appropriate scowl with his fingers, at which point I would burst out laughing at the hilarity of it all. Prior to age eight my son's school pictures showed a boyishly innocent smile. The following years his demeanor was more serious, calculated to achieve the austere male gaze. He no longer wanted to be innocent.

When my daughter was four, she was playing with her dolls while the neighbor girl, Molly, rifled through my daughter's jewelry box, stuffing her necklaces under her leotard. My daughter thought Molly was her best friend. She was innocent.

I lost my innocence when I divorced. When after twenty years love turned to hate. When for two years the machinery of the court system was levelled against me, as my husband tried to take my children away to assuage his guilt. I am no longer innocent.

I am no longer surprised by the evil men do to each other. What I am surprised by is innocence. That innocence still exists in spite of it all. That innocence is worth protecting.

## Discouraged

When I was two I remember sitting on a vast green lawn covered with yellow leaves. My father had been hired to rake the leaves and had brought the whole family along to help. I was too little to hold a rake, so I sat with my legs stretched out in front of me with my ankle- high brown lace-up shoes on. There is a picture of me frowning on that lawn. I remember looking at that endless green span and all those leaves and feeling overwhelmingly discouraged at the task. I didn't see how my father could ever rake all those leaves. I don't remember there being an end to it.

When I was five my family would go to the Drive In to see a movie on Saturday nights. I remember well the sinking feeling I would get when the movie showed nothing but men on the screen. Men with black suits and hats with Uzis. With nothing but men on the screen I knew nothing good would ever happen. There would be shooting and killing and car chases and endless arguing and talking. Men discouraged me as nothing else could.There would be no pretty dresses, or smiling faces, or warm arms of love, or sweet scenes with animals. The animals would all get killed. The men would have to win, and to win there would always have to be a war. Everyone would suffer. Because of the men having to win.So when I determined that we were at a movie with nothing but men on board, I would promptly lay down in the back seat and fall asleep. It was preferable to the discouraging movie.

Years later at ten I was on the YMCA swimming team. My main rival was a girl named Judy Miller whose mother held the stopwatch. We were at a swim meet, and I had just touched the wall, finishing the race, coming up to see Judy Miller still swimming towards the wall. I had won the race but the judges announced Judy Miller as the winner. She was presented with the gold medal.

The next day I was sitting on our front stoop with my head in my hands. Our swim coach came up to me and said I should have won the gold medal. But it was too late. I was discouraged. I saw how the world worked. If your mother held the stopwatch, you won the race. Simple as that.

When I was thirteen I was in a sledding accident. I nearly died from internal bleeding. I had been in the hospital several weeks recovering from surgery and made it out of the ICU to a recovery ward. I had been there long enough to recognize the routine, and one morning I realized I had not been given my breakfast. I rang for the nurse, and she confirmed my worst fears. I was going in for another surgery that morning. Hadn't the doctor told me? I said no as tears sprung to my eyes and rolled down my cheeks. I thought I was through with all that. No breakfast. I should have known.

A few years later, my parents had a bitter divorce. We children fled in frightening secrecy with my mother to live in a dinky duplex. My father came home to an empty house and an all-encompassing rage.

After enough time had passed, we were allowed to see our father again. He took us to his dark apartment. There was nothing to do there, so I idly opened the refrigerator. The sight discouraged me more than the divorce itself. There was nothing but milk in the refrigerator. An army of milk cartons lined up to do battle with his ulcer. His hopelessness engulfed me. I never went there again. Some despondencies are too deep to share.

A Chance

One Saturday after Christmas in 1961 I was in a near fatal sledding accident. When I woke up in the ICU I was concerned that I might miss the history test scheduled for the next Tuesday. Not only did I miss the test, I didn't go back to school until the following September. Since I was in the eighth grade I wasn't able to try out for cheerleader, or Folk Dance Club, or any of the fun extracurricular activities available to ninth graders. I had missed my chance.

Midway through ninth grade the Student Council announced that there would be a Talent Show for anyone interested in auditioning. I thought, "This is my chance." My chance to show the class I was back. I hadn't been completely erased by my accident. I loved to dance, so I made up a dance to the theme from "The Sundowners," an Australian movie. The dance was simple: the sun rising, turning into day, the sun setting, falling into night. I asked my best friend, Elaine Parker, to do the dance with me. We rehearsed in our living rooms every day. We donned our costumes of red tights, red turtlenecks, and orange scarves draped around our necks. We performed our dance for the school. I was happy. Our dance was a success.

The next year passed, and I found myself once again erased. This time by a move to Tacoma, Washington from Colorado Springs, my beloved home. My mother had married a man from Tacoma. I started eleventh grade knowing no one. I was invisible.

When a school Talent Show was announced, I thought again, "This is my chance." To say, "I'm here." To say, "This is who I am." I performed my dance to "The Sundowners" alone in my red tights, heart pounding. Later that day, on my way to English class my teacher asked me where I took ballet lessons. I told her I'd never had ballet lessons. She said, "You should take ballet from Jan Collum."

I went home and begged my mother to sign me up for ballet lessons at Jan Collum's. It was my chance to seize ahold of something that I had dreamed of. Something that came naturally to me. Something strong. Something beautiful. Something expressive. That's what dance was to me for the next thirty years. I became a choreographer. I was a dancer. I took my chance with "The Sundowners," and it paid me back a thousand fold.

# Regret

It was the first day of junior high school. The route had changed for walking to school. Bitsy, Sissy, Sally, and I walked past Linda Dana's house to pick her up.

Linda had been my friend throughout grade school before I had met Bitsy, Sissy and Sally. Linda lived with her mother and older brother in a small unkempt house surrounded by a brown lawn. Their house was dirty. The toilet in the bathroom was orange from rust. The dishes on the shelves in the kitchen were covered with a layer of dust which looked like thick grey snow. Linda's clothes had holes in them. But none of that had mattered to me because Linda and I had fun together. Riding our bikes with the wind whipping our ponytails we had gone on adventures, exploring. Intrepid.

But Linda's house and the holes in her clothes mattered to Bitsy, Sissy and Sally whose fathers were doctors and who lived in tri-level ramblers on cul de sacs with manicured lawns tended by a gardener.

At my request and to the other girls' consternation, we stopped by Linda's house to gather her to walk to school with us. Linda came out and started walking with us. Bitsy noticed the holes in Linda's white sweater. She reached for a strand of yarn and started pulling. Sissy and Sally laughed as she did so.

Linda, keenly aware of their disdain, retaliated with a sharp, "Well, you don't have to unravel my whole sweater!"I was mortified and thought Bitsy, Sissy and Sally were cruel, but I didn't speak up to defend Linda. I deeply regret my silence that day. Linda deserved better.

Linda never walked to school with us again after that day which I hope was a reflection of a healthy self-esteem.I remain ashamed of my paralysis.

# Anger

I live alone. I never get angry. No one pushes me into a corner from which I must lash out to escape. No one infringes on my freedom, my autonomy, my self-esteem causing me to defend myself uselessly. No one suggests I am crazy for having an opinion which differs from theirs or acts patently superior to me in every fundamental way. No one tells me what to do or forces their will on me unwelcomely. But it was not always that way.

I remember a day when my hands shook with rage, and anger filled my head like helium fills a balloon. I was in a car with my mother and sister, my stepdad and his son, a Hell's Angel, his little sister, and the slobbering dog. We were near Bakersfield, California in 95 degree heat crossing the desert. We were united in one aspect. No one wanted to be in that car.

As we drove across the fiery desert, my stepdad had his left arm dangling out the window turning redder and redder. The skin bubbled up in blisters which he would pop open and then peel the skin off, layer by layer. As disgusting as it was to watch him do this, what he said about doing it was even more disgusting. "This is fun for me," he gloated.

I was a quiet, serious sixteen year old who had just been uprooted from what I deemed paradise, Colorado Springs at the foot of Pikes Peak, to Tacoma, Washington suffused with the smell of Sulphur from the paper mills. Not a day went by that I didn't marvel at the low level to which I had sunk, living with a Hell's Angel who slept with his motorcycle next to his bed, put his muddy boots on the kitchen table where we ate, and communicated with monosyllabic grunts. Not a day went by when I didn't wish to see a crystal blue sky overhead instead of a constant dull gray drizzle of rain. And now here I was crammed in the middle of the back seat, carsick, with the dog's drool running down my neck. By mid-afternoon we were in the middle of nowhere when my stepdad pulled the car over and told us to get out. He went to the back of the car and came back with a rifle. It was time for some redneck bonding.

One by one we were summoned to shoot the gun. The Hell's Angel went first. Glad to have anything to do with explosives, he aimed and fired. Then came my mother. I couldn't believe my innocent, church-going, nonviolent mother would pick up that rifle but she did. Then came my sister who also did as she was told.

I was sitting leaning against a rock reading a book. My blood was surging in revolt. I was hardly breathing. I vowed I would never shoot that gun. His daughter was the only person left, and then it would be my turn. I panicked and tried to calm down, stared at the words in front of me.

Then it was time. I heard my name. I said sweetly, "No thanks David, I'll just read my book."

I had always been a pacifist. Guns to me were instruments of murder used to kill innocent creatures like the delicate deer in the mountains or my boyfriend's father who was murdered. I wanted nothing to do with killing or the guns used to do it.

I remembered one horrible day when I went to my best friend's house to play and saw a beautiful doe strung up by her hooves hanging from the back porch. It sickened me. I didn't see how my best friend could have boasted to me, "See what Daddy got?" How could she have been proud of that?

I heard my name again. This time lower, more insistent. "Louise! Get over here!" His authority was being challenged, and he had a redneck's response to that.

My heart was pounding. I tried to seem impassive but inside I was seething. My hands were shaking. Three more times I declined politely.

He upped the ante, threw out an ultimatum. "We're not leaving here until you get over here and shoot this gun!!!"

I could see that it was true. We wouldn't leave. They would keep on staring at me, waiting for the obstinate child to acquiesce, the tension building until darkness fell. We would still be waiting there, in the middle of nowhere, with that fat man peeling his skin away, waiting for time to start again, waiting for me to shoot that damn gun.

Finally, my mother could stand it no longer, and she said apologetically, "Just do it."

Vanquished, I put my book down. Got up. Walked over to where he stood holding the gun. Raised the rifle. And shot the gun.

His authority restored, now we could leave and time would go on. But I would never forgive him. He had violated me to the core, and decades later, I would refuse to go to his funeral.

## Things My Parents Made Me Do

The all-time worst thing my parents made me do was drink Watkins liniment when we were sick. It tasted so awful that if it didn't make you sick, it would surely scare the sickness right out of you. When I got older I realized it wasn't meant to be ingested. It says right on the bottle "For External Use Only." It was what farmers would rub on their animals for sore muscles. To this day I shudder when I recall the taste of that liniment going down my throat.

The next worst thing was only being allowed to use two squares of toilet paper. My father would yell at us to enforce this edict. My mortified sister would fold her two squares diligently trying to achieve some necessary thickness, but two squares is not enough to wipe yourself clean. I now keep at least sixteen rolls of toilet paper in my house, and I use as much as I want thanks to Daddy.

My mother made us put a dime in a jar every time we called our brother or sister "stupid" or "dumb." We only received 25 cents allowance a week so we couldn't afford to say it more than twice a week. If our mouths continued to offend my mother would wash them out with soap. She would wet a rag, dip it in Ivory Soap Flakes, and jam it in between our resistant teeth. I was impressed by how strong she was in those moments, as she pried open my jaws to stick the foul rag in.

We were all raised in sturdy shoes. Instead of pretty patent leather Mary Janes, I wore ugly brown leather high tops. Instead of sleek, cool sandals it was thick-soled saddle shoes. That's why years later, I always wore heels even when gardening or playing soccer with my son. It was ridiculous, but I would have my revenge.

My sister and I weren't allowed to open bobby pins with our teeth. Threats were made as prophylactic to our doing so. My father would warn, "I just saw two sisters whose teeth were all silver from opening bobby pins with their teeth. They had to have all their teeth pulled out and replaced with silver teeth." This didn't have the desired effect, however. We continued to open bobby pins with our teeth, except when he was present, and neither of us have silver teeth.

In our house children were to be seen not heard. We were forbidden from putting our feet up on the couch. Feet remained firmly on the floor. And there was no jumping on the bed in childish glee. Glee itself was absent in our household.

When I became old enough to be vain about my appearance, I was forced to wear flannel-lined jeans under my dresses to school if it was cold, which it was all winter long in Colorado. I was humiliated by the bulky jeans sticking out from under my skirt and would take them off in the bathroom when I got to school, ashamed to let the other kids see them.

As children we were taught to say "Please" and "Thank you" religiously. My father would drive me places, while taking the opportunity to vent his rage to a captive audience, yelling at me all the way there. When we arrived at our destination I would say sweetly, "Thank you for the ride," as if it had been a pleasant experience. Daddy never saw the irony in that.

We weren't allowed to eat potato chips or drink coke or soda pop, because, we were told, it would eat holes in our stomach. Now my cravings for a salty snack are indulged shamelessly, although I still don't drink coke.

We each had chores, and it was my responsibility to dust everything. I would start with the living room, go to the dining room, and then the bedrooms. My brother had a model airplane collection that he had made in his bedroom. I dusted that, too. That night at dinner he came into the kitchen furiously accusing someone of breaking one of his model airplanes. I didn't remember breaking anything, but I got the rap. He told me never, ever to touch any of his stuff again, and I was happy to oblige.

In the home I made for my children glee became a definitive option. My children and I danced with abandon causing the dog to riot. They roller skated in a big circle through the house laughing wildly. Their friends came over every day to play and made as much noise as they wanted. Music echoed off the walls. My daughter at age three clomped proudly through the house in shocking pink satin scuffs with green and blue rhinestones on them. No sturdy brown shoes for her.

# Girlfriends

My first friend was acquired under nefarious circumstances. I was the new girl in the second grade at Steele School. A girl who lived on my block was walking me home down an alley. There was a tall yellow brick wall running the length of the alley behind which stood a matching yellow brick mansion. The girl said her uncle lived there and that he killed little girls by chopping their heads off and throwing them off the top of Pikes Peak. She knew because she would see their bodies with ants crawling all over their necks on Sundays when she and her family went skiing. I was terrified. Then she told me she would tell her uncle not to kill me if I would be her friend. Grateful not to be slaughtered, I said I would, thus marking the beginning of an ill-fated friendship.

A more benign grade school friend was Linda Dana. We would perform tricks on her rusty backyard swing which was a tetanus shot waiting to happen. But we didn't care. In our minds we were glamorous circus acrobats dazzling our audiences with our daring. We went exploring, riding our bikes to Austin Bluffs or Monument Valley Park. The spirit of adventure lived in us, and we planned to own a horse ranch together when we grew up.

In the sixth grade I became very close to a girl we called Sissy. We wrote lengthy epistles to each other every day detailing our innermost thoughts. Our boyfriends were best friends, and the four of us did things together, like walking through the empty sewers hand in hand. Sissy and I went on a marvelous vacation together to the Great Sand Dunes, rolling down the dunes together laughing. The sand in our hair, our eyes, our noses, everywhere.

In junior high I developed a crush on my new best friend, Elaine Parker. She had a boyfriend who was two years older and was always worried about the hickeys on her neck and what her mother was going to say,or that her boyfriend was going to get tired of her and drop her. She had very thin lips and for some reason I was envious of them. We would stand in front of the mirror in the girls' bathroom ratting our falling hair and putting on lipstick. I would stare at her thin lips and wonder how I could get my plump ones to look like that. I envied everything about her, her lips, her cheerleader big sister, her other best friend, Janelle, her boyfriend, Eddie.

In my twenties I met Marilyn at ballet class in Los Angeles. We studied under the notorious Carmelita Maracci and became fast friends. Marilyn was a free spirit. She told me once that if you were walking down the street and had to step up onto a curb, it could be really difficult if you didn't really WANT to step up on the curb. That was the thing about Marilyn, you couldn't make her do anything she didn't want to do.

I remember cringing when she said she used to stick pins in her gums just to feel the sensation. My five year old son heard that. I wished he hadn't.

Marilyn used to spit cake into a milk carton with her daughter when they wanted to celebrate instead of swallowing it. She didn't want to get fat but wanted the cake anyway.

Marilyn's daughter was sick for many years and died shortly before Marilyn moved to Seattle. She told me once that if I had been her daughter's mother she would have lived. There was this vast difference between us. I was practical. Marilyn was passionate. I had a job. Marilyn lived off of welfare. I had two blooming children. She had the ghost of an Infanta. Marilyn was effervescent. I was realistic. I had the ability to step up onto the curb when I didn't want to. Marilyn couldn't do that.

Sadly, my heart has been broken as many times by girlfriends as boyfriends. My daughter's babysitter became like a sister to me. Every day we had long confidential talks. One day without provocation she informed me that she was taking stock of her life and that I could no longer be a part of it. I felt as rejected as if by a lover. Versions of that same scenario would happen two more times in my life where I had a cushy cozy relationship with a girlfriend and she would turn her back on me without looking back. Girls can be as fickle as boys.

I met the friend of a lifetime in Jewel when I went back to the university after my divorce. We were intellectual equals and loved discussing our classes, professors, and ideas which we were studying in the Women's Studies Department. Our lives ran like parallel tracks to the same destination. We loved to go out to eat together indulging our taste for fine food and wine at our favorite restaurants throughout the city.

Jewel expressed her creativity through building. She could do electricity and plumbing as well. But she was most noted for being Wenatchee's Apple Blossom Queen, and a more regal queen I have never seen. Our families became one and the same. She loved mine and I doted on hers. We commiserated on the joys and sorrows of motherhood, grandmotherhood, and mentorship.

Jewel was eccentric. He wore only cerulean blue down to her underwear and shoes. Her apartments were decorated in blue, and you couldn't give her a gift that wasn't blue. I gave her a blue cloisonné elephant once and she got rid of it because it had red flowers on it.

I discovered the city of Chefchaouen in Morocco that is all blue. Blue doors, blue houses, blue streets. I told her, "I found your city." She never got to go there. She died from the coronavirus after being the best friend for thirty five years that I could ever hope for.

# Jobs

When I was eight my first job was selling Girl Scout cookies. I felt so grown up dressed in my uniform, taking the money, handing over the cookies, making change. We were in competition with other girls in my troop to see who could sell the most boxes. One girl's family was rich. They bought all of her cookies and gave them away at the country club. I thought it was unfair. I went door-to-door selling a box at a time, or worse, being rejected and selling none.

When I was ten I helped my father deliver telephone books for 50 cents an hour. He would drive the car, hand me the telephone books and tell me where to take them. The worst part about that job was the vicious barking dogs guarding some houses. Then my father would intervene, rolling the phone book into a club to chase the dog away. It was the only time I recall him being protective.

I babysat, also for 50 cents an hour, as a teenager of course but nothing steady.  At sixteen I got a job at People's Department Store teaching calisthenics at a charm school. I had visions of taking over the aging charm school proprietor's place, a dream she did not share.

At the same time, I took a job as a Luzier's saleslady. Luzier is like Avon and sells cosmetics door to door. My patient mother drove me clear across town to innumerable training sessions in which I memorized verbatim the spiel that they give about each product. I remember going to a classmate's mother and her listening with rapt attention as I parroted about exfoliates and clarifying lotion. She humored me and bought a lipstick. It was a pity sale. I continued going door to door unsuccessfully. I am not a natural born salesman. I am not pushy and I don't override people's natural reticence.

In college I waited tables at a German pastry shop. Dressed in a dirndl I proudly carried the pastry tray featuring Shwartzvelderkirschtorte. Customers said I looked like Alice in Wonderland.

At nineteen I became a cocktail waitress at the Athens Café notable for Medea, the middle aged belly dancer, and Sheila, the transvestite fellow waitress. For this job we wore Roman tunics which were one-shouldered and very short. Maria, the owner, insisted that Sheila show me how to fix my bra while wearing it. I wasn't keen on Sheila, who had a deep bass voice and was clearly a guy, seeing me in my bra and fiddling with my strap.

I'll never forget the night when Sheila's mother came in for a drink. Sheila sat down next to her, and they were like two pillars of salt. Sheila and her mother both with matching hair ratted up to the ceiling in beehives, dressed in long evening gowns, sitting with their backs to me like pristine Gothic sisters. I thought it was so odd. I wondered, "How does her mother introduce her? 'This is my daughter Sheila?'"

On New Year's Eve Medea didn't show up for her floor show, so Maria had Sheila put on Medea's costume and belly dance.  Sheila did the best she could with her narrow hips shaking and her broad shoulders undulating to entertain the Greek sailors, who were so drunk they didn't seem to notice she was a man.  Now transvestites get their own TV show, but back then they were unheard of.

I was a dancer and a choreographer, and for the next thirty years all my jobs would be teaching or performing dance. That was a job I loved, was born for, felt inspired by, and gave my heart and soul to. Then one day a lady backed her car into my kneecaps pinning me between her car and mine and put an end to my dance career. So I became an English teacher.

I taught creative writing and critical thinking for Northern Arizona University on the Navaho Reservation. That was a good job if only for the 20% discount it afforded me at the trading posts on the res where I stocked up on turquoise jewelry.

The most impressive thing about that job was the 600 mile per week drive, circling the entire state of Arizona, I had to make. The drive nearly killed me, and every week I had to do it to make it home to Flagstaff for the weekend.

After that I became an international traveler teaching ESL in Taiwan and Japan for five years. I fell in love with Japan, not so with Taiwan although they had good street food.  Taiwan was notable for the black mops drying outside everyone's house, mops as black as if they had tarred the roof, but they were used for cleaning. That said something about the city I lived in.

By then, I was used to being the only white person in the room, but my enthusiasm for my job had dwindled to the necessity of making a living. I worked for ten years teaching refugees at Refugee Women's Alliance before I said goodbye to the world of work and completed the path I'd .travelled since I'd first asked, "Would you like to buy a box of Girl Scout cookies?"

Color

My first memory of being surrounded and embraced by color was when I was four, and my mother made me a red coat with a circular skirt. Standing on a chair while my mother pinned up the hem saying "Turn…Turn…" I felt myself enveloped in red.

My father also loved the color red. He would make the whole family pose for pictures holding up garments that were red that they weren't actually wearing, making for the geekiest photos you've ever seen.

Red was his passion. We would be driving down the highway and he would spot some red aspen at a distance. We would stop, get out, and hike to the glowing cherry red trees where he took more pictures.

Red continued to fascinate me throughout my life. In my early twenties I had a pair of red heels that I wore everywhere, dancing and even gardening in them.

At Pow Wows I collected exquisite red beaded hanging hair ornaments which draped across my bedroom until the rueful day I put them into a suitcase with all my other treasures and threw them into a dumpster for safe-keeping. I was delusional.

In Taiwan I discovered delicate red Chinese embroideries in an antique shop and hung them on the walls of my room. I was surrounded once again in red. The red of Chinese and Indian brides.

When I entered junior high I was very fond of pale pink, the paler the better. I had a pale pink fuzzy sweater that itched. I wore it anyway, because it made me feel feminine. Later that pink would become known as ballet pink which was the color of the tights and ballet slippers that I would wear for thirty years as a dancer.

I was in high school when I came to like green. I went to Betty Radonich's Charm School where we learned how to walk up and down stairs, how to pluck our eyebrows, and what colors looked good on us. For this lesson we held up squares of different colored fabrics up under our chins and surveyed the results. I learned that my best color was forest green, and never to wear tan. I promptly went and made a forest green wool dress that, I felt confident, showed me at my best.

I love the green of Christmas trees, set off by the twinkling lights. The green of the pine forests of Flagstaff, Arizona which are so fragrant that when you get off the airplane there and inhale your first breath you wonder, "What is that intoxicating scent?" Pine.

When I was sixteen I walked by an old decaying, abandoned house that was the deep dark brown of weathered wood. I came to love the color brown because of that mysterious house. I made myself a soft brown deep wale corduroy jumpsuit that I wore with pride. When my boyfriend asked me what my favorite color was, I said, "Brown." He thought I was crazy. But I still think the brown of wood and the brown of earth is beautiful. How better to set off the color of a flower?

As a young woman I went through a white phase where I had a whole wardrobe of white antique lace clothes. I choreographed dances and costumed them in all white. I learned to Tat and made ribbons of lace with the white thread. I hung white curtains at all my windows and loved to see the light shining through the white cloth.

After my divorce my closet was mostly black. It was slimming and calming to me. My financial advisor, a delightful big-haired blonde, dressed all in black. She eventually killed herself. After that I quit wearing so much black.

Blue will always be the color of my best friend, Jewel, who wore only cerulean blue down to her shoes and underwear. Her home was a showcase of bright blue glass. She painted her van blue. She was a sailor and loved the blue of the sea. I loved the blue of Colorado's skies. Looking into the intense blue of infinity.

Now my thing is embroidery. I like looking down and seeing a whole palette of colors on the clothing I wear. I love color and looking at a set of 120 gradated colored pencils all lined up next to each other excites me. I draw because of the chance to utilize all those bright beautiful colors.

# Clothing

When I was a toddler I had a yearning to wear the sunsuits which were hanging in the closet that had fit me when I was a baby. This was the beginning of my hunger for clothes which intensified when I grew older.

At five my babysitter, Grace Hill, an old German woman, made me a beautiful blue velvet dress with a scalloped neckline and a checked cobalt taffeta skirt. I felt like a movie star in that dress and wore it every Sunday to church.

My mother was a seamstress and made all our clothes, so early on I had the pleasure of going to pick out fabric for the play clothes, dresses, and nightgowns she would sew for us. I loved looking at row after row of bolts of colorful cleverly printed fabrics. I learned by sight and by touch to identify corduroy, seersucker, dotted Swiss, gingham, plaid, wool, cotton, flannel, organza, chiffon, taffeta, satin, twill, lace, broadcloth, chintz, silk, and the quintessential velvet.

As soon as I could, I learned to sew and was enamored by and tried my hand at all kinds of needlework: knitting, embroidery, drawn work, smocking. I loved spending careful hours making something special and unique. I made a pink gingham sundress with a painstaking border of drawn work embroidered with Fleur de Lis, and a turquoise wool sheath with a smocked yoke. My older boyfriend said I looked FINE in it. I was transported by his sexy compliment and loved the dress that had inspired it.

In high school I made all my own clothes including a faux leather trench coat and a brown corduroy jumpsuit that I thought were really cool. When bell bottoms came into style I made elephant–legged pants out of pin striped wool which I thought were audacious.

I started sewing clothes for an English designer named Pauline Conboy who owned the boutique called Maggie May. We worked together during my college years, and she designed while I made my wedding dress out of a turquoise and gold sari.

When I lived in Los Angeles, fashion central, I purchased a pair of Superstar pants for my five-year-old son. These were a pair of denim overalls with an elaborately decorated red velvet heart covered with rhinestones and silver brads. He loved wearing his Superstar pants and I hung them on his bedroom wall after he grew out of them.

I decorated all our bedrooms with clothing. A red silk embroidered Chinese wedding gown in mine. A toddler's lavender and green appliqued Chinese suit in the baby's room. Rainbow colored Korean dresses in my daughter's room. The beauty and diversity of clothing from around the world fascinated me.

Clothing and clothing construction has continued to interest me throughout my life. In Taiwan I discovered and collected contemporary clothes that were decorated with ancient Chinese embroidery. In Japan I discovered shibori which is an intricate dying technique used on kimonos and scarves. The Japanese also love pleats, and there are entire stores that sell only pleated clothing. The American tradition of T-shirts and jeans demoralizes me. I don't even own a T-shirt or jeans.

As a dancer I made all of my costumes, and as a dance teacher I would churn out 120 skirts every 12 weeks with matching scrunchies for my students' recitals. Sadly, after downsizing from a six bedroom house to a one bedroom apartment, I no longer have my sewing machine. I miss it. There is an empty hole where once there was a jumbled mess of fabric scraps, scissors, needles and pins, tissue paper patterns, measuring tapes.

But I still admire well-made clothing. The feel of a skirt swishing around my ankles. The loving details someone in some far away country still puts into making a dress or blouse so we can enjoy wearing it. A designer I currently feel passionate about is Johnny Was. He creates profusely embroidered garments that are not for the faint of heart. They are expensive. I'm saving up.

# Courage

At a young age I became aware of what courage was required to be my brother. He was five years older than me, and I looked up to him. But beyond that it took great courage to be a boy in my family. My sister and I had our mother to emulate, and she was a good mother. But my brother had only my father to look up to, and he only gave an example of how not to be.

My father had a violent temper, and he was paranoid. His favorite address for his children was "dirty stinking rotten carcass." His words were seared into our brains like a firebrand.

I remember when my brother was ten he was late to scout camp. The whole family had loaded into the car to take him to camp two hours away in the mountains. Obviously if my brother was late, it was the fault of the parent who drove the car. But my father blamed my brother and yelled at him all the way there berating him mercilessly. I remember thinking my brother was brave after we got to the camp, as he ran down the hill ready to face the music for being late.

In High School my brother went to music camp where they evaluated him on the saxophone. I remember him cheerfully reporting to my mother that the judge had said he had a vibrato that sounded like a nanny goat. I was impressed that he took this criticism in stride as it would have deflated me.

When my brother was sixteen he stood up to my father one Christmas. My father had been yelling at him for God knows what reason, and my brother challenged him to a fistfight. I couldn't believe the courage it took forhim to stand up to my father's rage. They went outside and had it out. My father was a little meeker when he came back in. My brother had become a man.

At the University of Colorado my brother went into the school of engineering and started flunking out. My father's torrent of words rained down on him centering on "Ignoramus." Unperturbed my brotherchanged his major to what he excelled at-music- and went on to get straight A's.

When my brother married and had twins, one of them had Down's syndrome. My brother never bemoaned the fact but threw himself into becoming the best advocate for a special needs son as he could. My nephew never learned to read but with endless patience, persistence, and hope my brother taught him to read music by color coordinating the notes. My nephew learned to play pieces on the recorder, my brother would play duets with him. They performed in churches and senior centers giving my nephew an aura of professionalism which he never would have had without my brother's devotion.

One night while walking home my brother was struck by a car and killed, cutting short a life he had lived with courage in the face of all odds.

# Denouement

The girls were having fun. Troop 289 was sledding on a crisp afternoon three days after Christmas at Monument Valley Park. It was Linda's turn. She laid down on the sled and went sliding down the slope steering away from the trees. At the bottom she got off and pulled the sled back up to the top of the hill. Then it was Louise's turn. Rita begged to go with her, so Louise laid down first, and Rita got on top of her. They started down the mountain. Trees went whizzing past. Then the sled seemed to establish its own course. It was headed straight for the trunk of a tall tree. The watching girls were screaming, "Steer! Steer!"

Louise was steering as hard as she could to no effect. Rita rolled off as the tree trunk loomed. The sled reached its inevitable destination. Louise smashed into the rock solid tree trunk. Denouement.


She was meticulous about fixing her hair every morning. She would line up the two mirrors, one in front, one in back, until she saw a never ending row of mirrors with her hairdo sandwiched in between. It was a high donut shaped bun with a single tendril cascading from the middle of it falling in a perfect curl.

She walked to school early every day to meet him in the library before school. He was a senior. She was not. She wrote his name over and over on her notebook copying his signature.

He had asked her to the General Palmer Ball. She couldn't believe it. All she thought about was the General Palmer Ball.

Her mother agreed to make her dress. She chose pink chiffon over yellow taffeta. She wanted to look like a Peace Rose. She watched the progress on this garment with anticipation.

She was ashamed of their house, a small duplex where she and her mother and sister lived, so she wrangled an invitation to a young couple's house which was a modern split-level on the night of the ball. He would pick her up and return her there. It was an improvement.

Throughout the day at school she would walk a certain way through the halls in order to pass by him.

In World History she would sit in her seat on fire from thinking about him.

On the day of the ball she showed up in the library wearing a turquoise smocked sheath she had made. He said she looked "fine." She was ecstatic.

The night of the ball she wore her Peace Rose dress, but he didn't mention it. She looked sweet, not sexy, a fatal mistake.

At the ball she remembers being introduced to his friends, the captain of the football team and his date, the head cheerleader. She might as well have been introduced to Tom Cruise. She didn't know what to say after hello. They looked at her as if she didn't exist. For them she didn't.

She remembers walking across the dance floor and asking the band to play "The Way You Look Tonight". They lied and said they didn't know it. He didn't like her doing that, that small show of independence. He stopped talking.

He took her home early, walking her briskly to the door. She had the coldest feeling, as if the blood had stopped flowing through her veins. She knew she'd never see him again. Denouement.

It was Thanksgiving. A wife was going to prepare the traditional turkey dinner with all the trimmings. She was in her husband's office, cleaning. Her husband was a musician. She began straightening up his cassette tapes. She picked up one which had her husband's handwriting on it. It said, "Taken." Next to it was another tape in the same handwriting which said, "Orgasm." She had a bad feeling. She decided to listen to the tapes. Her hands were shaking as she pressed "Play." It got worse. She heard the sounds of sex on the tape. Her husband's sounds. Then a woman's voice that said seductively, "I think this has gone far enough." But there was no cessation. Then her husband's voice saying, "You've been a great help. I mean, I couldn't have done this without you." The sound of fucking continued. Her heart had stopped. It all came clear. Her husband's latest concert, "Tango Diablo." The black haired woman who always wore sunglasses who had been occupying all her husband's time. His obsessive photographs of her.

She thought back to the night she went to his concert with her son, naively expecting to be proud of her husband. Then her confusion when listening to the sounds of sex while onstage her husband covered his mouth with his hand and laughed. Now the discovery of the tapes made it all clear.Denouement.

## Gifts

I was given four tests by Native Americans which I gratefully passed. The first occurred at Taos Pueblo, the oldest continually inhabited structure in the U.S. I was attending a retreat at the nearby Mabel Dodge McLuhan House and went one summer day to see the Pueblo. I walked into an adobe room where an old man was bent over some drums he was making. As he was absorbed in what he was doing, I didn't interrupt him. Eventually he turned, surprised that I was there. His words struck me as high praise, "You walk like an Indian."

A few years later at Taos Pueblo, I had gone to ride horses up to the top of Taos Mountain. The father of a ten-year-old boy directed the boy to guide me to the top. The boy clearly did not want to do this, but sullenly had no choice to accept. We rode slowly up the mountain, the boy bitter at his lot of taking a white woman up the mountain. When we got to the top he asked doubtfully, "How good a rider are you?" I answered, "Good." He took it as license to plunge headlong down the mountain at breakneck speed. We careened down, rocks flying, on no path, the horse's eyes wild with fear. I gripped my horse tightly with thighs made of steel from dancing. Every once in a while the boy would look back at me, incredulous that I was still on my horse. When we finally made it down to the stables, he had a wicked grin on his face. The white woman had passed his test.

Years later I was at a Pow Wow browsing the arts and crafts. A beautiful young Indian woman saw me and said, "For you I will show you this." She reached under her table and pulled out a bundle which contained a magnificently beaded gourd rattle. I was honored that she had shown it only to me. No price was too high for that sacred talisman. Before I left she looked at me and said seriously, "Be very careful with it." I assured her I would. That beautiful rattle has been in a place of distinction on my mantle for thirty-five years. When I die a young woman who is a poet and earth-lover will inherit it. It will continue to be cared for carefully after I'm gone.

In 2001 I was teaching on the Navajo Reservation in Rock Point, Arizona. Bennie Begay was a student of mine. One day in class Bennie gave me a picture of himself clinging like a tick to the back of a furiously bucking bronco. He had won the 1998 World Championship bareback riding title. The next time I saw him I reciprocated and gave him a photo of me backlit while performing in a dance concert. There was an equity between us remembering past glory.

After centuries of abuse and mistreatment by white men, these gestures of acceptance were the most precious gifts to me.

# Time

When you're a child a year seems like forever. Measuring from five to six years old, or from one Christmas to the next, feels like facing infinity. As a child telling your age was significant. You were five and a half, not five, or six and three quarters, not six.

As a naughty child, you get a Time Out. Time spent sitting in a chair or standing with your face to the wall in a corner. Then seconds tick by so slowly. Without a diversion time comes to a halt, forgetting you completely without your myriad interests to keep you going.

In school watching the hands of the big clock on the wall, waiting for the bell to ring the end of the boring period, time crawls as slowly as a snail.

In the hospital in pain minutes seemed like hours, and I had to use props to get time to keep moving. Otherwise, it might stop altogether leaving me in a hell of suffering. The prop was the TV, and I counted time by how many thirty minute TV shows it would take to make it to my next morphine injection. The short-lived bliss the shots delivered made my life bearable, made time move on, and made me ultimately heal. The visits once a day my mother made to the hospital marked time for me. I would listen for her footsteps coming down the hall in the afternoon. This rendered another day passed in what seemed like a lifetime spent in the hospital.

As a mother, time is measured by the ages of your children. When Jason was five...when Elektra was born...These provide the standard units by which all other events are calculated.

In middle age I was so busy there was never enough time. I always had more things to do than could possibly be squeezed into a day. I hurried from one activity to the next accomplishing dozens of things before fixing dinner at night.

On the Navajo reservation I measured time by the decomposing carcass of a cow. The first day, on my way to work as I breezed past Lukachukai in my Toyota Corolla, I noticed a dead brown and white cow lying by the side of the road. Every week as I drove by that cow there was less of it, until finally, there was nothing but the dry white pelvic bone lying Georgia O" Keefe style by the highway. A year had passed.

Eight seconds was all it took to make Bennie Begay famous. Eight seconds on the back of a furious bucking bronco, and he was the World Champion Rodeo Star. Eight seconds, rather than a college education, would make him a renowned teacher at Rock Point High School. Eight seconds made him a hero to the sulking Navajo juniors, the hopeful Navajo seniors at Rock Point. Eight seconds changed Bennie Begay's life.

When I am absorbed in something I love to do, such as writing a story, drawing a picture, or choreographing a dance, hours fly by like minutes. Going with the flow brings such complete satisfaction and joy that time loses its grip, and I float in time unaware of its usual tyranny.

As a retired person, I have open-ended time. Days are long and activities are scarce. Getting the mail is an event. The length of time it takes a child to grow up constitutes a generation. By the time your grandchildren have children, time is calculated by generations.

When meditating, in solitude, or in peace, time becomes generous and all-encompassing, surrounding us with goodness and blessing. Time's fullness and richness is showered on us.

Music plays, dances, and seduces us with time. Tempos andante or allegro entice us to match its languor or perspicacity. As a dancer I made love to the legato, chased the pizzicato, and rose on the crescendo. Music is the master of time, causing it to heel or get cracking at a whim. Music takes us back to times past which were once loved by our younger selves in times gone by.

In old age we are aware that time is fleeting. We don't remember our age, having to calculate back to the year we were born and add up. We just get used to writing one year on our checks and the next year appears. We wait for time to run out as it did for my best friend, Jewel, who died from the corona virus. We know that our days are limited, and that makes time precious. All we really have is time. Savor it. Enjoy it.

## Music

The first song in my life was "This Little Light of Mine" which I would sing holding my finger up, promising not to hide my light under a bushel.

Time moved on and in sixth grade I was slow dancing to "Mr. Blue" and "Lonely Boy." So sad. So romantic. I wanted them never to end.

In the hospital at thirteen after a near fatal sledding accident, I was given my first transistor radio so I could tune into KJR and listen to the hits every day. I loved to listen to the rousing sounds of Tijuana Brass and the sexy bossanovas like "The Girl from Ipanema."

In the ninth grade "West Side Story" transfixed the nation. The perky "I Feel Pretty" became every girl's coming of age song. The sassy "America" spoke for the rebel in me. And the beautiful "Maria" soothed me into a dream state.

In college I listened to "Farewell Angelina" by Joan Baez, and "Girl from the North Country" and "Corinna, Corinna" by Bob Dylan until I drove my roommate crazy with the repetition. I, on the other hand, could never get enough.

After that it was Joni Mitchell and The Beatles because where would the sixties be without them?

I married a musician who composed music to the dances I choreographed. We lived, breathed, and ate music. My husband loved jazz, and we often listened to "Water Boy" by Don Shirley. He also was into Joao Gilberto, Stan Getz, and The Eagles. There was always music playing in our house.

After I was divorced I couldn't stand to hear lyrics of love or heartbreak in English, so I started listening to world music in languages I couldn't understand. My favorite was Guardabarranco, a brother sister duo from El Salvador who wrote their own lyrics and sang beautifully together. I also liked Native American bands such as Walela and Kashtin, and Sharon Burch's "Yazzie Girl" sung in Navajo.

I listened to blues when I was dating a gentle astrophysicist who had a picture of Anne Frank on his bedroom wall. We listened to Muddy Waters and Nina Simone savoring the deep mellow songs.

As a dance teacher for thirty years I collected music from every genre to appeal to my students from children to adults, from classical to rock. I singlehandedly kept the music publisher Ladyslipper in business for decades by ordering twenty cassettes at a time. Discovering new musical treasures within the pages of their catalogue was a thrill to me.

Who can forget the celestial sounds of Enya? I would lie in bed surrounded by candles listening, believing myself to be in the company of angels.

I loved Tracy Chapman and her "Fast Car" and "Talkin Bout a Revolution.' I want to have Tracy

Chapman's "All That You Have Is Your Soul" played at my funeral. That will make the soundtrack to my life complete.

## Children

On the happiest day of my life I woke up at 6:00 AM and baked blueberry muffins. By 9:00 I was having strong regular contractions. We went to the hospital and were shown into a room where a woman who had been in labor for 48 hours was screaming. I asked myself, "Is that going to happen to me?" It didn't. I didn't scream. Six hours later my beautiful baby boy arrived. I squeezed the nurse's hand with all the love I was feeling. From that moment on I was in love with my son.

Jason had golden curls and a golden smile. Every morning when I went in to his crib to get him up, he would smile that smile that would light up the world. I would pick him up, happy to be his mother.

As a toddler Jason loved to put on his father's boots which came up to Jason's crotch. Then he would put a hat or a bucket on his head, and I would take his picture. He loved to draw and would spend hours with his big sketch pad and magic markers drawing hundreds of fish. Little fish in schools swimming away from BIG fish with their mouths open wide, teeth threatening.

When he was five the first Star Wars movie made a big impression. He drew epic scenes from Star Wars documenting Princess Leia, the Jedi Knights, Hans Solo, Chew Baca, Luke Skywalker, and Darth Vader. I still have a big drawer full of these dramatic drawings. His passion. Followed by BattlestarGalactica, another muse.

Jason went to Montessori school and was learning his numbers. He made a number roll which is a roll of paper like a roll of toilet paper on which he wrote numbers beginning at one and going up to millions. His number roll was eight inches across and still growing. We lived on a hill. One day while getting out of the car Jason dropped his number roll. It swiftly rolled down the hill unrolling all the way. I ran after it laughing hysterically.

In sixth grade Jason won the Seymour Kaplan Award, given to the student who most exemplifies humanitarian values. He had a wonderful teacher named Nahnie who became one of my best friends.

Ten-year-old Jason loved to ride his bike. He bought bike parts at a special shop in Bellevue which enabled him to do tricks which he would practice after school.

In junior high Jason got a paper route. Then he got two paper routes. He would get up at 4:30 AM to roll the mountain of papers on our living room floor. Then he would deliver the papers on his bike. He was quite the businessman. It was the start of a successful career.

He had beautiful long blonde hair and wore it braided, in a ponytail. In high school he started working at Maneki's, a Japanese restaurant. He learned to cook tonkatsu, pork cutlet served with cabbage. He was surrounded by girls. The girls from Garfield, his school, andthe Japanese girls who lived with us. He drove an old classic car that was always filled with his friends.

His best friend was THE Rob, who was taller than Jason. These boys were Taller (my son Jason at 6'2") and Tallest (THE Rob at 6'5'.) Two beanpoles, they would lounge on the couch with beatific smiles on their faces. Happy with themselves and their young promising lives.

Jason went to college in Japan. He got accepted at a notorious dormitory called WakaiJuku and attended Sofia University in Tokyo. He went by himself, courageous, optimistic, full of love for Japan and the possibilities offered by freedom in an exciting big city. He was no longer a child. He was a man.

After I had my son, Jason, I said to myself, "I'd like to do that again in ten years." And that was just what I did. When I was pregnant the second time, the baby was very active with lots of sharp kicks and restless nights. I had a strong intuition that it was a girl, and I named her Elektra to go with her electric personality.

I went to the hospital to have a Caesarean, because she was a breach baby. After examining me the doctor said, "I don't mean to tell you what you're having, but I felt a scrotum." I didn't believe him. I was sure I was having a girl. I had already written poems to her.

I had the Caesarean, but it brought catastrophe. The doctor had severed the main artery to my right leg without realizing it and stapled me back up. By the time he had operated again to see what had happened, I had nearly bled to death. When I woke the next morning he was at my bedside in tears.

After a week I got to take my beautiful daughter home. She had a head full of dark glossy hair, and she held her hands clasped under her cheek for the photographer who came to take pictures.

After I healed and got back to dancing, I would take Elektra with me to rehearsals. I had a basket bassinet whose edge I had wrapped in blue, green, yellow, and peach ribbons, and she would sleep cozily there. My dancers were charmed by her beautiful, expressive moon face.

At Christmas I made her a felt stocking to hang on the fireplace. Jason's stocking had a yellow sun on his. I put orange lightning on Elektra's.

One sunny summer day she sat on the grass singing, "Honey loves the flowers, Honey loves the grass. Honey loves the trees." I called her "Honey" and for a while she thought it was her name. She was the inspiration for many love poems I would write.

When she was three our family was severed by divorce. My husband sued for custody, and the court dictated a schedule which divided my children's lives between mother and father. They had the fortitude and resilience to manage this dislocation.

Elektra had "the terrible twos" at three. She would throw tantrums in stores, screaming for not just one but two dolls. I lived in fear of going shopping with her. Later her choir director said about her beautiful singing voice, "I know where that came from," alluding to the tantrums. It was a price I gladly paid to hear her sing. Her voice was as clear as a diamond, and she sang with confidence.

She joined The Northwest Girlchoir when she was six and sang with them until she was eighteen. Every Christmas and spring brought a wonderful concert of beautiful heartfelt songs.

In grade school Elektra made friends easily. Her first being in kindergarten with a sweet African boy named Yves. Then came Wen, a Chinese girl, who was her best friend for years. A posse of girls would gather at our house to play after school or on the weekends. They would play My Little Ponies, dolls, dress-up, or act out scenarios with rose petals from our garden. Like The Babysitter's Club, the girls were Elektra, Wen, Ashni, Calli, and Melanie. They are still friends thirty years later.

Elektra loved to swim, unlike her brother who insists I gave him "drownding lessons" when he was little. I took her swimming at the Seattle Club where her little head bobbed up and down behind a barbell float while she swam. One day she held the barbell in her teeth and her tooth came out.

In the sixth grade Elektra also won the Seymour Kaplan Humanitarian Award. But the undisputed highlight of that year was going to see a Boyz to Men concert with Calli. Elektra and Calli spent the whole day getting ready. They curled their hair, they did their make-up, they picked out their best clothes. They looked polished as pearls when we drove to the Tacoma Dome that night.

In high school Elektra wrote beautiful poetry, she learned to drive her own car, and she spread her wings on a trip to Italy. But her good friend Calli was killed in a car crash involving a car full of kids who'd been drinking. It was heart-breaking. Elektra's best friend, Jeremy, helped her get through it.

She fell in love with Michael Helde at Garfield. They were in Tribes, a theatre production, together and shared a passion for boxing.  After graduation they went their separate ways. Elektra went to San Francisco and Chile for college. Then she and Michael met again and married. She was no longer a child. She was a woman.

# Hands

My Mother's hands. Kneading bread, covered with flour, rolling out a pie crust. My Mother's hands ironing. Smoothing the hot fabric on the board. My Mother's hands sewing and teaching me. Holding the seam open with her index finger. Her round, unpolished nails a testament to working class.

My Father's hands. Framing a picture. Sanding the board. His broad thumb once nearly cut off by the hungry Sabre saw. His long little fingernail assiduously grown. Hands whose touch I grew to fear.

My brother's hands. Fingering the keys of his golden saxophone. Hands creating music from notes on a page. Hands carefully gluing parts of a model airplane. An airplane I broke while dusting with my careless hands.

My sister's hands. Nails bitten down to the quick. Bleeding. Playing jacks. Twosies and threesies. Playing Monopoly. Convincing me to sell her Park Place. Hands practicing to become a secretary. A helper's hands.

Startling white hands with long tapered nails painted red of a third-grader's mom. Hands delicate and manicured. Hands that had not been working. Kept hands. So unlike my Mother's hands, always busy.

Holding hands. The first sign of romance. My hand with Pat Gaughan's ID bracelet on it. Proud. Chosen.

My obstinate hand. Holding a coke through the whole movie, so the boy I didn't like couldn't hold my hand.

Hands, the vehicle for love. Petting Goldie, my Grandmother's beloved old collie.

Hands, the vehicle for wonder. A black and white calf sucking on my fingers. His toothless mouth as soft as velvet.

My husband's big warm hands. We photographed our hands entwined on the top of Mount Rainier among the wildflowers. He would reach for my hand when we were walking. I felt protected, loved in his enveloping hand.

A pianist's hands. My husband's hands created moonlit landscapes, classical storms, tropical lagoons, heavenly paradises. His magic hands could materialize audible worlds, could communicate, could transport, could poke fun. He would not wear a wedding ring, because it would interfere with the webbing of his hand.

A dancer's hands. Expressive. Employed in every mobile instant. Reaching for infinity. Stretched with angst. Softening for lyricism.

My hands, as a mother. Conveying love, peace, serenity to a crying infant. Smoothing circles on their back. Patting up the burp. Folding the endless soft white squares of diapers.

My daughter, Elektra's, ceramic hand. Her finger's splayed in surprise. Stopping time at first grade.

The pastor's wife's hand in church. Caressing her sulky daughter. I knew what that hand felt like. Giving confidence, giving courage, giving forbearance.

Trembling hands. My Grandfather's hands holding a teacup. Shaking uncontrollably. My hands writing the insurance information after a car accident.

Brown knotted Navajo hands. Weaving their Creation Story out of horsehair. Beading a sacred gourd rattle to dance with at Pow Wow.

Consoling hands. My son, Jason, holding my hand when I was having a breakdown. Scared. His hand saying, "You're not alone."

Hands. The key to drawing, painting, signing, cooking, baking, woodworking, carpentry, building, playing music, playing games, gardening, knitting, crocheting, beading, embroidering, sewing, writing. Thank hands for all these things. Hands are beautiful. Old hands are noble. Young hands are full of promise. A baby's hand grasping your finger. A tiny hand with five tiny pearl nails is strong.

## About the Author

Louise Salisbury grew up in the Rocky Mountains of Colorado. She was a professional dancer and choreographer for thirty years, maintaining her own company called Dance Connection. She has a Master's degree in Teaching English as a Second Language. She was an ESL teacher in Taiwan, Japan, and Seattle, Washington, for fifteen years before retiring in Seattle. She is mother to a son and daughter, and grandmother to six grandchildren. She likes to draw, write, read, and dance.